Medieval Joke Poetry

A Ángel
en un fin de semana
de mudéjares en
Ithaca,

Benjamín

HARVARD STUDIES IN COMPARATIVE LITERATURE

FOUNDED BY WILLIAM HENRY SCHOFIELD

50

Medieval Joke Poetry

The *Cantigas d'Escarnho e de Mal Dizer*

Benjamin Liu

Harvard University Department of Comparative Literature
Distributed by Harvard University Press
Cambridge, Massachusetts, and London, England
2004

PRINTED IN THE UNITED STATES OF AMERICA

FIRST PRINTING

ISBN 0-674-01663-7 (cl.)
ISBN 0-674-01664-5 (pa.)

Library of Congress Control Number: 2004109983

This book is printed on acid-free paper, and its binding materials
have been chosen for strength and durability.

CONTENTS

Acknowledgments

This book would not have been possible without the generous support of a number of institutions and individuals. Andrew W. Mellon Fellowships from the Woodrow Wilson Foundation, the Jacob K. Javits Fellowship from the U.S. Department of Education and grants from Harvard University, the Real Colegio Complutense at Harvard, and the University of Connecticut Research Foundation were instrumental in supporting both the research and writing phases of the project. I gratefully acknowledge the Department of Comparative Literature at Harvard and the Harvard University Press for their willingness to see it into print. A version of chapter 5 previously appeared in *Queer Iberia: Sexualities, Cultures, and Crossings from the Middle Ages to the Renaissance,* edited by Josiah Blackmore and Gregory S. Hutcheson (Durham: Duke University Press, 1999), 48–72. A version of chapter 6 appeared, in Spanish, in *Erotismo en las letras hispánicas: aspectos, modos y fronteras,* edited by Luce López-Baralt and Francisco Márquez Villanueva, Publicaciones de la Nueva Revista de Filología Hispánica, 7 (México: El Colegio de México, Centro de Estudios Lingüísticos y Literarios, 1995), 203–217. I am grateful to the editors of both volumes and to both presses for their kind permission to publish those chapters here.

I owe a special debt of gratitude to my mentor Francisco Márquez Villanueva and to Jan Ziolkowski for their invaluable guidance and encouragement at every stage of the project. It is a privilege to acknowledge those whose generous comments and suggestions have greatly improved the manuscript: Joe Blackmore, Luis Girón, Louise Vasvári, Joe Snow, George Greenia, Sam Armistead, Greg Hutcheson, David Nirenberg, Mary Gaylord, Simon Doubleday, Denise Filios, Frank Albers, and Regina Llamas. I also thank the many other friends and colleagues in Cambridge, Connecticut, Kalamazoo, and Madrid who took the time to read, hear, and respond to the early drafts and chapters. I am grateful to Susan Hayes and Kathy George for their part in editing and preparing the manuscript for publication. "Por fazer romaria, pug' en meu coraçon, / a Santiag', un dia. . . ." I am indebted to many colleagues in Spain and Portugal for generously sharing their time and expertise, for which I thank Darío Villanueva, José Luís Rodríguez, Francisco Nodar Manso, Americo Lindeza Diogo, José Luis Couceiro, Mercedes Brea, Camilo Flores, Juan Casas Rigall, Milagro Laín, and Juan Paredes.

Finally, my heartfelt thanks go to my wife, Carmen, to whom I dedicate this book.

Medieval Joke Poetry

INTRODUCTION

A Poetry of Jokes and Intention

With impious words, he mixes
a joke and a curse . . .
[mezcla en palabras impías
un chiste a una maldición.]
— José de Espronceda 100

The best part of telling a joke, runs a joke that means the opposite of what it says, is explaining afterward what made it funny. So to explain: this joke is about the crucial element of timing; to retain an effective force, the joke's wit must become apparent in the proper moment and context, to the right listeners. Without timing, the artless joke falls flat, losing the punch, spontaneity, timeliness, and appropriateness of its humor. Or perhaps its meaning is closer to what E. H. Gombrich writes, in response to Freud's *Jokes and Their Relation to the Unconscious*, about verbal ingenuity as a paradigm for art:

> [A]ny attempt to translate a verbal joke is doomed to failure. To use traditional terminology, the joke simply does not permit us to separate form from content. . . . To "interpret

[dreams]" could only mean to put them into words. But what the theory of art, to which Freud approximated the theory of the joke, teaches us is precisely that this type of interpretation will never be possible; one can never put into words what a work of art "says." (107)

What untimely hope then can there be to find humor in explaining, commenting, translating, or interpreting jokes whose punch line was delivered not moments, but centuries ago? Or is it now possible only to labor to unearth their meaning and to explain them, while at the same time abandoning all hope of fully recovering their peculiar and artful humor? This is one of the conundrums presented by the corpus of medieval *Cantigas d'Escarnho e de Mal Dizer* (*Songs of Mockery and Insult*, henceforth abbreviated CEM).

The CEM, composed by various authors during the thirteenth and fourteenth centuries in Galician-Portuguese, are joke poems. The corpus presents an extensive collection of burlesque, comic, and transgressive "counter-texts" (Bec) to the courtly and popularizing traditions of Galician-Portuguese love lyric. These satirical and invective poems are classified, a bit misleadingly, by a fourteenth-century *arte de trovar* in the *Cancioneiro de Biblioteca Nacional* (CBN) according to whether their critiques, insults, or abuse were aimed directly ("descubertamente"), as in the *cantigas de mal dizer,* or indirectly by means of words with multiple meanings (*aequivocatio*), as in the *cantigas d'escarnho:*

> The *cantigas d'escarnho* are songs made by the troubadours in which they seek to speak ill of someone and say it through covered words that have two senses in order that they not be understood [lacuna in ms.] easily. And learned men call these words *aequivocatio.*

> [Cantigas d'escarneo som aquelas que os trobadores fazen querendo dizer mal d'alguẽ ẽ elas, e dizê-lho per palavras

cubertas que ajã dous entendymentos pera lhe-lo nõ enten-
deren . . . ligeyramente. E estas palavras chamã os clerigos
hequivocatio.] (D'Heur, "L'*Art de trouver*" 103)

José Luís Rodríguez has shown in concrete instances how this figure of
double meanings, *escarnho,* or, to use its learned equivalent, *aequivocatio,*
forms the "stylistic nucleus" of the *cantigas d'escarnho.*

Mal dizer, by contrast, means simply "to speak ill of someone" without attenuating the language through double meanings, often in the form
of direct obscenities:

> The *cantigas de mal dizer* are those that the troubadours
> compose [. . .] openly about whatever they are speaking ill
> of, containing words that have no other meaning besides
> that which they plainly signify. . . .

> [Cantigas de mal dizer son aquelas que fazẽ os trobadores
> [. . .] descubertamente, ẽ elas entrã palavras a que queren
> dizer mal e nõ aver outro entendimento senõ aquel que
> queren dizer chaamente. . . .] (107)

The combined label *cantigas d'escarnho e de mal dizer,* found in the
manuscripts and adopted by subsequent editors, indicates that the two
styles are not mutually exclusive and are in fact often combined in individual *cantigas.* It also points to the extreme heterogeneity of the texts that
make up the collection, which range from playful and highly ingenious witticisms to invectives hurled in the most degrading language. The compilation of the corpus began in the Middle Ages as a general counterpoint to
the two genres of Galician-Portuguese love lyric: the courtly *cantiga d'amor*
and the popularizing *cantiga d'amigo* (Lanciani and Tavani, "Cantiga de escarnho e maldizer," *Dicionário*). The CEM are thus something of a catchall,
a hybrid category of texts that in some way resist categorization.

Roughly speaking, the texts date from the beginning of the thirteenth to the mid-fourteenth century. Their production and preservation were fostered in the courts of such royal patrons as Alfonso X of Castile, the Learned King (ruled 1252–1284) and his grandson Denis of Portugal (ruled 1279–1325). Both of these figure prominently as authors as well as auditors and patrons, among a diverse company of noblemen, courtiers, and professional entertainers (Ackerlind 105–151; Tavani, *A poesía* 255–267).

The period of these texts' production witnessed the large-scale military, political, and cultural consolidation of the territorial gains of Reconquest, which culminate in the taking of Seville in 1248 (Castro 150–151). Pero da Ponte, who is after Alfonso X the most prolific author in the corpus of CEM, offers a panegyric on this occasion to the victorious King Fernando III of Castile, father of Alfonso X, that begins "O muy bon Rey, que conquis a fronteyra. . . ." In the praise poem, Pero da Ponte exalts the conquest of Seville above all other conquests "in all three religions" ["en todas tres las leys"], that is, Jewish, Muslim, and Christian, indicating the new consolidation of religious and cultural communities under single political rule (Pero da Ponte 109–111; Alvar and Beltrán 158–160). Alfonso X, as successor to Fernando III, inherited the riches of the newly conquered territories, peoples, and cultures, as well as the complex tasks of administering and appropriating them (Jackson, chap. 3, "Thirteenth-Century Conquest and Synthesis"; O'Callaghan 14–18).

The analysis of the CEM's "fossil" jokes resembles the interpretation of archaeological traces, seeking to impart meaning to the cultural life of former societies. It cannot restore the soul of wit to the jokes, but can only allow their remains to reveal a partial narrative about a time and culture that would otherwise remain forever unseen and foreign behind the screen of historical distance.

Only this process of incrustation has allowed outside access to these jokes, since memory and oral traditions fail when circumstances no longer permit the joke to be told: either when the subject of the joke is no longer popularly known, or when a certain turn of phrase or slang upon which the joke depends has already fallen into disuse. The study of jokes then becomes not simply analysis but itself also a parallel process of compilation; every study of wit is in turn a specimen case thereof. The analytic principles of Freud's *Jokes and Their Relation to the Unconscious* (1905) are illustrated by, if not based on, a number of witticisms by Lichtenberg, Heine, and others, along with contemporary reports of various wits and an ample collection, especially of Jewish jokes, carefully compiled and recorded. Anthropological studies of jokes in a Freudian vein, or in response to his writings, such as Alan Dundes's or Elliott Oring's, present themselves partly as compilations of folkloric material from the field, as it were, or rather from the shifting and evanescent field of language.

The "fossilization" of the CEM's complex and elaborate jokes is a threefold process. First the authors compose and frame their joke-poems as literary artifacts, in rhyming and metrical strophes, including both words ("razoẽs" or "dizer") and tunes ("sões") (CEM 175, 287). This first stage is one of poeticization (recollection *por rimas*), as the poems' technical artistry in performance attenuates the underlying jokes' tendentious force, that is, their directedness against a particular target and their intent to do harm. The formal technique of rhyme itself greatly resembles those types of verbal play that involve deformation, such as puns (paronomasia, *annominatio*) (Fried 83–99); though the jokes based on equivocation or homonymy more properly resemble the frequent Galician-Portuguese poetic technique of the *dobre*, whose doubling repetitions involve semantic play rather than phonetic alteration (Beltrán, "Dobre" 219–220). Poeticization further aestheticizes the verbal joke, the primordially social form of pleasure-producing economies of psychic energy, as Freud would have it, or of shared and hence social artistic "discovery," according to Gombrich: "a good joke is not an invention but a discovery" (105–106; Spector 118–119).

Next occurs textualization: the collection, compilation, and recording that belongs to the manuscript tradition, involving patrons, sources, and scribes. This aestheticization of the written word (recollection *por escripto*) obeys the motives of the *cancioneiro*, first likely undertaken according to author and later compiled into the (sparse) manuscript form under which the non-devotional lyric poetry in Galician-Portuguese is known (Tavani, *A poesía* 51–63; Oliveira 13–35). Finally, the textualizing process continues in the editing and commenting of these texts, motivated at times by historical interests, at others by linguistic, literary, national, or philological considerations.

But these interests lie principally in the texts, not in the joke from which they sprang. The joke itself is only transported and swept along by the fossilizing currents of poeticization and textualization, perhaps waiting, perhaps not, for the time when it will again become funny in the telling, rather than (*horribile dictu*) in the subsequent explanation. New times, new song.

The meaning of jokes petrifies when the social occasion of joke-telling and joke-listening disappears. Groups often define and set themselves against others, at times cruelly, by means of jokes, about another's or one's own ethnicity, gender, region, nationality, religion, dress, sexuality, social class, food, age, and so on. In this way jokes establish in-groups who "get" (both hear and understand) the joke against out-groups who are unable either to hear or understand it. Such jokes enable members of a group to identify themselves to and among other members of the same group. By so doing, the joke constitutes a culture's way of talking about itself to itself, naming itself, criticizing itself, criticizing others. "Laughter travels by neighborhoods," the Spanish proverb says ("la risa va por barrios"). These critiques are expressed indirectly, however, in ways that are articulated only through the multiple meanings arising from language that is equivocal, combinatory, substitutive, hybrid.

Within their elaboration of poetic language, the CEM combine the joke's kernel of verbal wit and the invective force of an underlying curse. The joke begins with a curse aggressively directed at someone in particular, an imprecation designed originally to injure. Verbal wit, however, by means of the joke-work that substitutes, condenses, and displaces in language, attenuates and suppresses the intentionality of this first impulse (Freud, *Jokes* 166–169; Madero 36–38, 44–45). Nevertheless, the satirical motive continues to underlie, and give a biting edge to the joke's more sociable senses in the poetry of *escarnho e mal dizer,* which in this way, like Espronceda's student of Salamanca, "with impious words, mixes / joke and curse" ["mezcla en palabras impías / un chiste a una maldición"] (100).

The combination is one very similar to the useful doubling described by Émile Benveniste of blasphemy and euphemism in such expressions as "parbleu" that both invoke in vain and conceal, also in vain, the name of God. In such altered expressions, Benveniste writes:

> The blasphemy subsists, but is masked by the euphemism that strips it of its expressive reality, and therefore of its ability to signify, by rendering it literally devoid of meaning. Thus nullified, the blasphemy makes reference to a profanation in language without going through with it, thus fulfilling its psychical function while diverting it and disguising it.

> [La blasphémie subsiste donc, mais elle est masquée par l'euphémie qui lui ôte sa réalité phémique, donc son efficacité sémique, en la faisant littéralement dénuée de sens. Ainsi annulée, la blasphémie fait allusion à une profanation langagière sans l'accomplir et remplit sa fonction psychique, mais en la détournant et en la déguisant.] ("La blasphémie" 257)

Similarly, the poetry of jokes of the CEM serves to divert and disguise the intentionality of invective, behind the euphemistic excuse that "it's only a joke." The tendentious joke deflects criticism of its intention, but conceals behind its playfulness a cruel will to injure. Were the joke to step out of its special zone of language games, it would no longer be a joke, but a source of insult and offense. In one Alfonsine *cantiga,* the king mocks a vassal who has refused to take part in the war against the kingdom of Granada of 1264 (Paredes Núñez, *La guerra* 14–15, 33–34), on account of his cowardice, as Alfonso alleges. Objecting to the seriousness of warfare (*armas e lidar*) and the possibility that it offers of personal injury, this noble protests that "it's not a game when someone weeps" ["non é jog' o de que omen chora"] (CEM 16). This rule that governs children's play humorously underscores the cowardice of the nobles who failed to heed the call of Alfonso's campaign, but at the same time its humor serves to allay the taste of bitterness in Alfonso's sense of betrayal.

Behind the curtain of wit and humor lurks a scene of painful animosities, anxieties, conflict, and contentiousness that must be covered over in language to avoid coming to blows or being driven to tears. Freud cites the case of gallows humor to show that "humor" is a social supplement to feeling, a gesture that opens out the privacy of personal emotion onto the public sphere of social participation (*Jokes* 283–287).

Another *cantiga de mal dizer* by Alfonso X el Sabio directly curses those same vassals who refused to take part in the war of Granada in 1264 (Paredes Núñez, *La guerra* 15, 38–39):

> He who crossed the mountains,
> not wanting to serve on the ground,
> now on the eve of war,
> > wants to know which way the wind blows?
> Since he now zigs and zags so much
> > Let him be damned!

> [O que foi passar a serra
> e non quis servir a terra,
> é ora, entrant' a guerra,
> > que faroneja?
> Pois el agora tan muito erra,
> > maldito seja!] (CEM 24)

The king's damnation not only recriminates the *ricomens* for their disobedience and their cowardice, but it also asserts the legitimacy of his authority over them, a power in this case specifically codified in the *Siete partidas* under the rubric "What treason is, whence it derived this name, and how many kinds there are" ["Qué cosa es traycion, et onde tomó este nombre et quántas maneras son della"]:

> The sixth [kind of treason] is, when anyone abandons the king in battle, or deserts to the enemy, or goes elsewhere; or leaves the army in any other way, without orders, before his time of service has expired. . . .
>
> [La sexta [manera de traycion] es si alguno desamparase al rey e se fuese á los enemigos ó á otra parte, ó se fuese de la hueste en otra manera sin su mandado ante del tiempo que debie servir. . . .] (7.2.1)

In the case of this *cantiga de mal dizer,* the question of whether the nobles' failure to observe law and custom merits punishment or forgiveness is rendered moot, because the ultimate effect of the curse ("maldito seja!") is not to negotiate the terms of retribution or redemption, but rather to affirm the king's very power to command, an issue no doubt very much on Alfonso's mind, given the acts of insubordination faced by him during his reign, as well as ingrained in the popular imagination (Juan Ruiz, 142–145).

Alfonso's *cantigas* thus respond in earnest to pressing matters of utmost concern, but through a mockery that is formalized in language. In the joking poetry of the CEM, the poet-king can turn as weighty a subject as treason into a verbal game, because only jokes can provide the supplement of humorous pleasure that, without violence, can stand in for violent emotions. The language of the joke brings into play its special capacities to deflect, transform, substitute, and condense into pleasurable forms of social exchange precisely at the most delicate, anxious, and conflictive moments that language would otherwise avoid as too explosive for ordinary words.

The link with Benveniste's pair of concepts, blasphemy and euphemism, goes even further, in the sense that the invective force of the CEM's "palabras impías" is likewise paired off, in a dialectic of praise and blame, against a pious poetics of devotion represented by the *Cantigas de Santa María* (henceforth CSM).

One of Alfonso X el Sabio's *cantigas de loor,* the songs of praise to the Virgin that decimally punctuate the CSM, delimits the boundaries of praise- and blameworthy conduct in a pair of alternating refrains:

> Cursed be he who will not praise
> her in whom all bounties are.
> [...]
> Blessed be he who will praise
> her in whom all bounties are.
>
> [Maldito seja quen non loará
> a que en si todas bondades á.
> [...]
> Bẽeito seja o que loará
> a que en si todas bondades á.] (CSM 290)

The refrains are interchangeable in form and in the incantatory style of their optative clauses, taking on in both cases the repetitive force not merely of a poetry of praise but of prayer. The limit that differentiates the blessing and the curse is of a moral order that lies only in the positive or negative valence of the syllables *bẽ-* or *mal-*. This dialectic of *laus* and *vituperio* gives equal time to extolling the proper and castigating the improper, because both complement and reinforce a recognition of the limits of behavior, between the exhortation "Do!" and the prohibition "Do not!"

It is indicative, however, that CSM 290, above, begins with a curse ("Maldito seja quen non loará / a que en si todas bondades á") whose double negation of praise only afterward modulates into the affirmation of a blessing ("Bẽeito seja o que loará / a que en si todas bondades á"). This type of reversal is typical of univalent discourses of co-optation, as, for example, in the redemptive sense of the proverb "no hay mal que por bien no venga" ["no evil comes save for some good" or perhaps "all's well that ends well"].

If the CSM represent a ritual of praise (*loor*) and benediction, the corpus of CEM enacts the contrary ritual mode of malediction, whether this takes the form of blasphemy, curse, invective, transgressive obscenity, satire, or deflected joke. However, whereas the alternating refrains of CSM 290 encapsulate an unequivocal dialectic of praising the good and blaming the bad, no such ideological complementarity exists in the hybrid and heterological worlds of the CEM, in which every turn of phrase can lead to another detour of meaning.

Pierre Bec argues, in his collection of Provençal "burlesque and obscene" texts, that these types of "countertexts" nevertheless collaborate to maintain in vigor the dominance of social and poetic codes:

> The "counter-text". . . is not ambiguous. In effect, it situates itself *within* the literary code, using its procedures to the point of exasperation, but fundamentally turning it away from its referential content. Strictly speaking, therefore, there is no ambiguity, but rather a deliberate juxtaposition, for playful or joking purposes, of a given literary code and a marginal, or even subversive literary code.

> [[L]e contre-texte . . . n'est pas ambigu. Il s'installe en effet *dans* le code littéraire, utilise ses procédés jusqu'à l'exaspération, mais le dévie fondamentalement de son contenu référentiel. Il n'y a donc pas d'ambiguïté à proprement parler, mais juxtaposition concertée, à des fins ludiques et burlesques, d'un code littéraire donné et d'un contenu marginal, voire subversif.] (11)

The poetics of the CEM differs in a crucial respect from these burlesque and obscene countertexts. To be sure, representation of marginal or even subversive referential content is found in the CEM, as in those texts. But the transgressiveness of the CEM lies not only in what they represent, but also the equivocal manner in which they do so, often playing about with the literary codes of other genres, but certainly not obeying or reinforcing them. The CEM are a poetry of "sins of language" ["péchés de la langue"] (Ramos 67–84), both for what they speak out loud and for the forked tongue of uncategorical equivocation with which they speak, disrupting at once conventions of the "what" and "how" of acceptable discourses.

The double transgressions of the CEM make for a highly restricted poetic audience, on one hand sophisticated enough to participate and take pleasure in the subtle equivocations and linguistic inventions of its wit, and on the other, sanguine enough to take pleasure in those "accursed words" ["palabras malditas"], "to whose magical ambiguity we entrust the expression of the most brutal and subtle of our emotions and reactions" ["a cuya mágica ambigüedad confiamos la expresión de las más brutales y más sutiles de nuestras emociones y reacciones"] (Paz 81). The very nature of verbal humor, that seeks out the peculiar zones of "magical ambiguity" in language and those moments when language is at its most inexplicable, tends to restrict it to a determined group — national, linguistic, or social — that shares not only a given language, but also a given way of speaking it. Because the joke must be shared with those who are also "in the know," humor points to those instances of peculiarity by which a culture recognizes itself. Humor is for this reason frequently taken as a touchstone of cultural participation.

There is a longstanding tradition of asserting the peculiarity of specifically Spanish humor, not simply of humorists who happen to be of Spanish nationality, descent, or language, but a special property of Spanishness, taken to be some amalgam or another of culture, nationhood, and language. Juan de Valdés, himself very conscious of both the political motor of language and of the unique linguistic situation of sixteenth-century Spain, had asserted as early as 1535, in his *Dialogue on Language* [*Diálogo de la lengua*], that the Castilian tongue was superlatively endowed for plays on words using double meanings or homonyms:

We have very many equivocal words and, what is more, although in other languages verbal equivocation may be a defect, in Castilian it is an embellishment, for with equivocal
words many very subtle and gallant things can be said in an
ingenious way.

[Tenemos muy muchos vocablos equívocos, y más os digo
que, aunque en otras lenguas sea defecto la equivocación de
los vocablos, en la castellana es ornamento, porque con ellos
se dizen muchas cosas ingeniosas muy sutiles y galanas.]
(126)

When Baltasar Gracián theorizes verbal and conceptual ingenuity in his
treatise on *Wit and the Art of Ingenuity* [*Agudeza y arte de ingenio*], he attributes a special cultural talent to the Spanish nation in this area of verbal play: "In Spain there was always freedom of wit" ["En España siempre
hubo libertad de ingenio"] (310). These arguments for a peculiar national
character, genius, or ingenuity, of course, may serve to align cultural and
linguistic traits with national borders that have been defined politically,
and so provide "natural" justification for these. If language is the "perfect
instrument of empire" (Greenblatt 17), laughter is by contrast an instrument of local self-definition: "laughter goes by neighborhoods" ["la risa
va por barrios"].

On occasion, the national parameters shift, but the accompanying
rationale remains largely the same. In Jorge Mañach's *Inquiry into the
"Choteo"* [*Indagación del choteo*], the national formation is that of Cuba
and the peculiar form of verbal humor, the *choteo,* is taken to be unique
to Cuba: a form "typically ours" ["típicamente nuestra"] (Mañach 11;
Pérez Firmat 53). Nevertheless, the argument made for linking idiosyn-
cratic humor and nationhood is very much the same as those made by
Valdés and Gracián. Likewise, the many collections of jokes, "secret" or
equivocal dictionaries (Cela, Criado de Val), linguistic taboos (Grimes
3–13), or even puns on proper names (Bershas; Martins 113–116) usually

lay claim to a form of cultural expression that is particular to the national or regional group in question.

The logic of inclusiveness and identification through humor and jokes also implies shutting out from certain possibilities of communication those who are unable to "get" the joke. This question involves much more than the issue of humor alone. Nevertheless, the general similarities of the claims made about the cultural specificity of humor point out one crucial feature of jokes: a desire to retell them, or failing that, to collect them and record them, which goes beyond the simple pleasure of the jokes themselves. Preserve these specimens of antonomastic wit, goes the reasoning, and a portrait of a culture, nation, and epoch will be preserved with them. The joke-book, like the songbook, is much more than a pastime, it is the self-portrait of a culture that issues a plea for remembrance in its own peculiarity.

Yet what the jokes and humor of the CEM equivocally represent are precisely the latent conflicts and divisions within society. The CEM constitute poetic utterances that are fundamentally and dialogically divided against themselves, explicitly so in the *tenço*, internally elsewhere. The linguistic ambivalence of the comic utterance produces a hybridization of discourses that M. M. Bakhtin has termed heteroglossia:

> Heteroglossia . . . is *another's speech in another's language,* serving to express authorial intentions but in a refracted way. [. . .] Double-voiced discourse is always internally dialogized. Examples of this would be comic, ironic or parodic discourse. . . . A potential dialogue is embedded in them, one as yet unfolded, a concentrated dialogue of two voices, two world views, two languages. (*Dialogic Imagination* 324–325; italics original)

The CEM require these double elements, voices, and worlds of language, to produce their artful and meaningful joke poems. First, the procedure of *escarnho*: the technique of verbal joking, turning on homonymy, wordplay, innuendo, and the semantics of multiple connotations by which the CEM so artfully construct their poetic *moqueries*. Second, the referential: the target of satire, the object of scorn, derision, and "speaking ill of someone" ["dizer mal d'alguẽ"], who is the intended target of the attenuated curse. There are no "innocent" jokes, as Freud terms them, in the CEM; they are all tendentious, directed, with a purpose.

Nevertheless, the apparent target does not alone constitute the meaning that the poem produces through its verbal play, or contrasting semantic fields, or shocking transgressions in language. These techniques of joke and language engender shifts and substitutions that reveal misgivings not only about the manifest targets of the *cantigas* but also about the latent anxieties arising from the jagged edges of social and cultural negotiations, which monologic normative measures such as the law inevitably fail to smooth over entirely.

In the works of other poets writing in the Iberian Peninsula both before and after the CEM, similar poetics of doubleness are discovered. Ibn Quzmān's prologue to his collection of Hispano-Arabic *azjāl* describes the layered senses and blending of opposites in his poetry, recalling the *Arte de trovar*'s definition of the *cantiga d'escarnho*. Ibn Quzmān writes: "I made [the *zajal*] close and distant, ordinary and strange, difficult and easy, concealed and obvious. . . ." ["Wa-ja'altu-hu qarīban ba'īdan, wa-baladiyyan ġarīban, wa-ṣa'ban hayyinan wa-ġāmiḍan bayyinan . . ."] (*Gramática* Ar. 1; Monroe, "Prolegómenos"). Of the many characterizations of the ambiguity of the *Libro de buen amor* (Dagenais, *Ethics* xiv), a very brief one will suffice here: Juan Cano Ballesta's rapid sketch of the Arcipreste's poetics of playful equivocation as one of "ambiguity, concealed double meaning and a carefree sense of boldness and irony" ["la ambigüedad, el doble sentido encubierto y la desenvoltura ironizante y apicarada"] ("¿Pretende casarse . . ." 9) could very easily be confused with that of the CEM.

All these cases of equivocal poetics in the medieval Peninsula, analogous with that of the CEM, surely correspond like it to ways of talking ambiguously, in speech that is alternately circumspect and unabashed.

These equivocal poetics of cultural ambiguity may represent, not just contrasting worlds of language that come together in jokes, but the very "impious" and "accursed" words spoken, out loud or under its breath, by a fractious society, divided and doubled within itself, at a decisive moment of cultural symbiosis in medieval Iberia.

1

PROPER NAMES, EQUIVOCATION,
AND *ESCARNHO*

[J]okes that "play about" with names often have an insulting
and wounding purpose, though, needless to say, they are
verbal jokes.

— Sigmund Freud, *Jokes* 107

At the root of the CEM's poetry of jokes lies a curse, and the curse is always an utterance directed against someone in particular ("dizer mal d'algūe ē elas"). As a communicative act, the curse requires as much a party against whom it is uttered as it does the one who curses; as a quasi-magical incantation that pretends to a power of a symbolic order, the target of the curse must be singled out, by name, for him to receive the full force of its invective. A joke built upon such a curse would be of the "tendentious" or purposeful variety, as opposed to the category of "innocent," unintentional verbal jokes (Freud, *Jokes* 107). The poeticization of the curse likewise softens its intention, as the directedness of the curse is somewhat attenuated and diverted by a supplement of "psychical energy" (in Freud's joke economy) or of aesthetic pleasure (Gombrich 105,

108–109). This combination of witticism and formal poeticization, so characteristic of the poetry of the CEM, holds it back from the aggressiveness of the unchecked and unequivocal curse. The CEM are, therefore, not only a poetry of jokes, but also a "poetry of intention," because they take aim at particular targets, but, by poeticizing their tendentiousness, pull the actual punches, or in other words deliver only symbolic blows, which can also sting, though they are only words. This cumbersome description of the process and its effects is necessarily roundabout, as is the characterization given by Freud in the epigraph to this chapter, because the tendentious verbal joke, which in Gombrich's formulation, cited above, may be the paradigm of the work of art, itself straddles the line between the act of communication and the playful discovery of aesthetic pleasure.

The definitions of the anonymous *Arte de trovar* point up the specifically personal targeting of both the *cantiga d'escarnho* and that of *mal dizer* (D'Heur, "L'art de trouver"): "dizer mal d'alguē." This means not merely to speak ill in general, as in the genre that Lapa and Tavani classify, after a Provençal fashion ("em maneira de proençal," to borrow Don Denis's phrase [Alvar and Beltrán 371–372]), as the *sirventés moral* (Tavani, *A poesía* 226–232). It also means to speak ill, publicly, against someone in particular, against the individual, usually by name, or if not, by proxy. The Galician-Portuguese joke *cantigas* are usually explicit in singling out the target of the satire. Many of the CEM begin with a vocative in the first line, calling out the name or title of the person against whom the poem is directed: Don Airas, Pero da Ponte, Don Gonçalo, abadessa, donzela, bispo, and so forth. Other times, the name is mentioned in the third person, when a brief report or notice is given as if in confidence to a second party.

By way of contrast, poetic treatises in the Provençal tradition censure this type of poetry of insult, which it classifies as *mal dig especial,* or *ad hominem* attack. Luis de Averçó's *Torcimany* (from Arabic *tarjumān,* "translator," "interpreter"; cf. Cast. *truchimán*), a medieval Catalan encyclopedic poetic treatise, explicitly cites the Provençal *Flors del gay saber* (Anglade 89) in condemning the use of this "defect" or "vice":

> Every troubadour should beware of this irredeemable vice, the *mal dig especial,* that is, no troubadour in compositions arising from this science [of poetry] should speak ill of anyone in particular, nor point out in satire any defect, vice or slander in another, as this way of speaking ill in particular renders its author dissolute and uncourtly. . . . All compositions in which this vice of *maldig especial* appears are held in contempt and considered highly defective.

> [D'aquest irreparable vici de *maldig especial* se deu gordar cascú trobador, ço es, que especialment negú trobador en los dictatz procehens d'esta sciencia no deu dir mal de neguna persona, ne maldient denotar algú mal o vici o difamació d'altre, com aquest mal dir especialment ret lo seu actor disolut e descortés. . . . [T]ots dictatz en los quals aquest vici de maldig especial sia vist, son fort menyspreatz e tengutz per greument viciatz.] (Averçó, 123–124)

The *Torcimany,* however, does give explicit permission to satires of social categories ("mal dir generalment") (124), after the manner of the *sirventés moral,* inasmuch as the "vice" lies in not in criticism itself, but in the criticism of particulars: "And on account of the aforesaid, it is prohibited to speak ill of anyone in particular, but in general terms it is permitted" ["E per tot açó demunt dit se defén a dir mal en especial de negú, e en general se permet"] (124). This is again entirely in keeping with the Provençal tradition as set out in the *Flors,* which describes the approved genre of the *sirventés* as a depersonalized "general satire to chastise those who think and commit evil" ["maldig general per castiar los fols e los malvatz"] (Filgueira Valverde, "La 'Seguida' medieval").

This, however, is clearly not the case in the Galician-Portuguese CEM. What to the Provençal tradition represents a minor style, included in the later *Flors* and *Torcimany* as if only for the sake of encyclopedic completeness, makes up on the contrary one of the three major groupings of Galician-Portuguese secular lyric. A glance through Pierre Bec's anthology of Provençal burlesque and obscene poems (relatively few when compared to the much larger number of courtly love lyrics and political *sirventés*) shows the Provençal tradition's comparative reluctance to name names and personalize invectives. A couple of the texts gathered by Bec, moreover, were produced by troubadours active in Iberian courts, and hence within the cultural sway of Galician-Portuguese lyric. At least one bilingual *tenço*, in Provençal and Galician-Portuguese, involves the Learned King himself in dialogue with a certain Arnaldo (Bec 157) and thus overlaps directly with the corpus of Galician-Portuguese CEM (CEM 430).

In part, the censure of the *Flors* and the *Torcimany* derives from the very postulate of their own composition, that rules can be set to prescribe the making of poetry, when the whole basis of a poetry such as the CEM — one of insult, mocking, and joke — is that it personalizes, against the generalizations of the subject of the law, and that it rebels against the explicitly signified strictures of the law. This transgressiveness defines the parameters of the "contretexte," the *mal dig especial,* and the component of *mal dizer* in the CEM. Even Alfonso X himself, who, as poet of *escarnho,* is one of the masters of the *ad hominem mal dizer,* in his role as legist in the *Siete partidas* is compelled to censure precisely these types of attacks, especially when they are fashioned in memorable forms of rhyme or writing:

> The evil which men say of one another either in writing, or in rhyme, is worse than that which is spoken in any other way by words, because if not lost the remembrance thereof endures forever, but whatever is stated in another way in words is soon forgotten.

[El mal que los homes dicen unos á otros por escripto, ó por rimas, es peor que aquel que dicen dotra guisa por palabra, porque dura la remembranza della para siempre si la escriptura non se pierde: mas lo que es dicho dotra guisa por palabras olvidase mas aina.] (7.9.3)

In some cases, however, circumspection proves the better part of valor and the person is not singled out explicitly by name. In these instances, where the target's identity is not disclosed, a title indicating social station, profession, or other sign of identity often stands in for the name, implicating an entire category of persons in the satire of a stereotype or caricature (Aguiar 65–89). Sometimes a poem will avoid overtly naming an individual who may be nonetheless clearly recognized by certain attributes (a lawyer who limps, a certain well-placed but near-sighted courtier). In a recurrent cycle of *cantigas* against lesser nobility, satires sometimes give their rank rather than name: *cavaleiro, infançon, ricome.* Alternatively, this can be substituted with the generic Don Foan (from Arabic *fulān,* "So-and-so"; Castilian *fulano*), where "Don" points out a certain social standing without specifying an individual. This cycle of CEM then represents a critique of an entire titled social class, though here manifested in such particularizing terms as personal habits, handicaps, stinginess, cowardice, or other moral or physical defects. On the whole, the comic effect of these *cantigas* pivots on the contrasts drawn between the privileges of feudal title and the expectations of a corresponding personal behavior. A nobleman who eats poorly on account of his own stinginess may be made ridiculous, but certainly not a peasant who does so out of bare poverty. Likewise, a nobleman who accepts the benefits of feudal vassalage, but then fails to render the service of his own obligations, represents another case of the comic failure to fulfill expectations. This is a type termed by Freud the "comic upon cathexis," in which the result does not coincide with the investment of imaginative energy to predict a reasonable outcome (*Jokes* 244).

Other groups of poems fit the same mold, but take aim at other social categories. A certain *donzela* may be taken to task for not meeting the social and literary expectations of the word used to characterize her sexual and social standing; for being unlike, even opposite, the courtly portrait of the morally and physically immaculate beauty (Rodríguez, "A mulher"). The CEM paint instead a negative counter-image of a flatulent and ugly *donzela* that is not desired by the lyric subject: "I do not desire an ugly damsel, / who farts before my door" ["Non quer' eu donzela fea, / que ant' a mia porta pea"] (CEM 7). Powerful intimates to the king ("Os privados que del-Rei an, / por mal de muitos, gran poder . . .") may be rebuked by characterizing them as being not loyal and discreet, but instead self-seeking calumniators and gossips (CEM 325).

From these displacements of personal invective to groups come the topical satires of classes, professions, gender, sexualities, ethnicities or disabilities that lend themselves to thematically or sociologically arranged studies of the targets of satire as a representation of society. But these types are rarely made fun of in isolation from each other. A single poem (in conjunction with others) directed against a particular individual may bring up in its equivocal manner of joking, say, in the case of Joan Fernández, the fact that he works in the field, along with the suspicious possibilities that he may be homosexual, of Moorish descent, physically "defective" (by circumcision) and ugly to boot (CEM 408). None of these really constitutes a satire of categories, but much more a use of such cultural stereotypes to heap as much abuse as possible upon a particular target designated by name.

The particularizing curse pertains to the realm of the verbal, where the function of pointing and singling out is performed by naming. The name-calling deals more with proper names than categories, since as Freud remarks, "jokes that 'play about' with names often have an insulting and wounding purpose" (*Jokes* 107). The tendentiousness of the joke on the proper name singles out a specific target because the proper name, in theory, is supposed uniquely and reflexively to correspond with the person that it designates. Like the Aristotelian definition of a "property," the name belongs only to one thing or person, and is convertibly predicated upon it (*Topics* I, 5, 102a17–19). When equivocation is brought to bear on the proper name, with intention, the joke is made not only about the name but about its convertible predicate, the person bearing the name.

An example serves nicely to illustrate the importance of the proper name to the equivocal poetry of the CEM. Once again, the CEM's word-play only rarely involves alterations in form, as in the case of nominal paronomasia or *annominatio* on personal names. Instead, these *cantigas* exploit duplications of sense that already exist within the name itself. Joan Airas de Santiago, in CEM 180, offers what is midway between a curse and a prayer against his homonymous namesake, Joan Airas. This impostor appears to be a *reedor* (barber); though this reading is not certain, it would imply a profession of humble station, along with tailors ("al-faiates"), furriers ("peliteiros"), and trumpet players ("trompeiros"), as another *cantiga* points out (CEM 287). In the refrain, our poet Joan Airas curses the other Joan Airas, exclaiming in a prayer or curse that is half-Satanic (in contrast to the prayers themselves, which are addressed to Nostro Senhor and Santa Maria):

> Whenever they call Joan Airas, the barber, I really think
> that they're calling me; but I pray to Our Lord
>> that the Devil take him,
>>> by whose fault they are taking my name away.
> They come by here calling Joan Airas all day long, and so I
> go when they call him, but I pray to Santa Maria
>> that the Devil take him,
>>> by whose fault they are taking my name away.

> [Quando chaman Joan Airas reedor, ben cuid'eu logo,
> per bõa fé, que mi chaman; mais a Nostro Senhor rogo
>> que atal Demo o tome,
>>> per que me tolhen o nome.

> Ven Joan Airas chamando per aqui todo o dia,
> e eu vou, quando o chaman; mais rog' eu a Santa Maria
>   que atal Demo o tome,
>   per que me tolhen o nome.] (CEM 180)

Lapa understands the latter phrase to refer to Joan Airas's "good name," or reputation as a troubadour. Joan Airas's more immediate complaint is, however, that he must inadvertently respond when people call out by name to the other Joan Airas, who seems to enjoy a greater popularity, by virtue of his profession, than does the poet. Joan Airas's *cantiga* seems thus to argue that his name should belong to himself alone, that is, that its signification, as a proper name, should be unique and hence unambiguous. The petulant assertion of (nominal) individuality entails a claim on the proper name as private property; and the recourse in prayer to the Lord and to the Virgin, as sources of divine justice, is akin to a legal defense of trademark.

Why is it so necessary for Joan Airas to assert the singularity of ownership over his name? As a poet of *escarnho,* he naturally would be especially attuned to the potential for satires based on just such fortuitous coincidences in language. But it also goes further than that. The existence of a homonym is the verbal equivalent of a double of oneself: it blurs the outlines of individual identity, and also those of property, of what it means for something to belong to someone.

"Property" as a logical relation is defined by Aristotle in the *Topics* as "a predicate which does not indicate the essence of a thing, but yet belongs to that thing alone, and is predicated convertibly of it." (102a18–20) Jacques Derrida, writing in "White Mythology" on problems of metaphor and categorization in the *Categories,* succinctly restates the Aristotelian position as it applies to the uniqueness of signification that characterizes the proper name: "A name is a proper name when it has only one sense. Or rather, it is only in this case that it is properly a name" (48).

Aristotle, it must be recalled, ends the *Categories* with a discussion of the everyday senses of the verb "to have," in an attempt to sort out the confusion arising from the multiple senses that a single word may possess (even here, the use of words for property, "having," and belonging is nearly unavoidable). Aristotle's discussion aims to dispel the possibilities of ambiguity in meaning of this fundamental verb, since any ambivalence in the laws of verbal property would render impossible the unique relations of signification necessary for naming individual things at all. This potential for confusion is exactly what makes up the "impropriety" of the CEM, both in the subject matter and in their equivocal manner of representing it.

Aristotle's *Categories* (and with it the traditional sequence of his logical works) opens with a discussion not of predicables themselves, but rather of the uniqueness of names. The problem here is not of essence, definition, or predication, but instead of signification, especially with the multiple significations that will prove to be so ubiquitous in the later discussion of the verb "to have." Laying down rules for "proper," unequivocal types of signification would seem to form a necessary preamble to the consideration of predication, logical categories, and ultimately to the discussion (that takes place in language) of logic itself. In this brief presentation, names are classified as equivocal, univocal, or derivative:

> Things are said to be named "equivocally" when, though they have a common name, the definition corresponding with the name differs for each. Thus, a real man and a figure in a picture can both lay claim to the name "animal"; yet these are equivocally so named, for, though they have a common name, the definition corresponding with the name differs for each. . . .
>
> On the other hand, things are said to be named "univocally" which have both the name and the definition answering to the name in common. A man and an ox are both "animal," and these are univocally so named, inasmuch as not only the name, but also the definition, is the same in both cases. . . .

> Things are said to be named "derivatively," which derive
> their name from some other name, but differ from it in ter-
> mination. Thus the grammarian derives his name from the
> word "grammar," and the courageous man from the word
> "courage." (*Categories* 1, 1a1–16)

Aristotle in fact uses the words *homonuma* and *synonuma* in senses, as is
apparent, that are not strictly equivalent to the English usage. But the
neo-Aristotelian tradition has long used the terms of Boethius's Latin
translation of the *logica vetus, aequivoca* and *univoca*. Aristotle himself
dismisses these apparently accidental convergences in language, regarding
them principally as a source of sophistical fallacies, which he treats in
much more detail in the *Sophistical Refutations* than he does in this prefatory part of the *Categories* (Edel 222–231).

The medieval interpreters of Aristotle expand, in both Latin and Arabic, on the definitions and examples given by the philosopher. It is possible to chart, as Françoise Desbordes and Irène Rosier do, the use of
specific vocabularies and illustrations in neo-Aristotelian traditions through
a number of later authors. Isidore of Seville, for example, condenses Aristotle's definition of homonymy into a single example of *aequivoca*. Instead of Aristotle's (possibly confusing) example, he gives the single
example of a lion: "a real lion, an image of a lion, and the constellation
Leo, are all called 'lion' " ["et verus et pictus et caelestis leo dicitur"] (vol.
1, 2.26.2).

Other scholars have also examined the specific interpretations given
in individual works, for example those concerning the "modes of signification" (Ashworth 85–101). Paul Vincent Spade distinguishes three principal modes of equivocation in the writings of William of Ockham, which
he terms equivocation "by chance," "by analogy," and "by context" (15).
The first type, "by chance," means convergence in the name of two otherwise unrelated things, as in the case of Joan Airas and his homonymous
barber, or between Isidore's "real lion" and the constellation "Leo."

The second type, "by analogy," is an equivocation of representation, in that both a man and an image of a man ("homo pictus") may be called "a man" or "an animal"; in Isidore's example, both the "real lion" and the "painted lion" are called *leo*. Other animals may be used at will: Umberto Eco demonstrated the concept with a plastic armadillo in a Norton lecture. Perhaps the best known literary example is an episode in Petronius's *Satyricon,* in which Encolpius jumps with fright when he mistakes a *trompe l'oeil* painting of a guard dog for a real one: "a great dog on a chain was painted on the wall, and over him was written in large letters 'BEWARE OF THE DOG'" ["canis ingens, catena vinctus, in pariete erat pictus superque quadrata littera scriptum 'Cave canem'"] (40–41). In Encolpius's overly literal reading of the inscribed text, "Cave canem," Petronius offers the wary reader a warning against the equivocal trap of mistaking representation for the real thing, painted dogs for real ones.

The comic effect produced by this type of equivocation through representation results from the difference in scale between the two levels of likeness that are joined by analogy. Encolpius's reaction, as if to a real dog, engages too great a movement for the reaction that is ordinarily provoked by paintings, as observed, for example, in a museum-goer. Out of this surplus of reactive movement, in Freud's conceptual economy of "ideational mimetics," is produced the comic laughter that responds to such contrasting, superimposed situations (*Jokes* 238–245; Spector 119–120).

The third type of equivocation, "by context," corresponds to what Aristotle meant by "synonymy," the use of the same term to describe different members of the same class, in his example, both a man and an ox may be called "animal." In many medieval logical treatises, Aristotle's synonymy comes to be considered, in logical terms, a subset of *aequivocatio*. Maimonides's precocious treatise on logic, reportedly written at age sixteen, the *Maqāla fī ṣinā'at al-manṭiq* (ca. 1151), synthesizes the tradition of Arab commentators into a comprehensive classification of the types of equivocation: he distinguishes univocals as a class of homonyms, distinct from synonyms proper, a term that he uses in the modern rather than the Aristotelian sense of the word (59). Equivocation "by context" then would be classified under his system as "univocal" homonymy. The precise correlations of

Maimonides's terminology with other systems are difficult to ascertain because this section of the work is preserved in Hebrew translations but not the original Arabic. Averroes had translated Aristotle's *homonuma* as *muttafiq,* meaning to be in agreement or similarity by convergence. This term is additionally glossed, similarly to Aristotle's text, with the term *muštarik,* meaning "sharing" or "common." In Averroes, it is not the things themselves, but their names (*asmā'u-hu*) that are shared or equivocal. Averroes has rendered *synonuma* as *mutawāṭi',* "agreeing" or "concurring" (the verbal form implies mutual action). Deborah Black has commented generally about "a tendency in the Islamic tradition, where the deception of the sophist tends to be linked primarily to linguistic equivocation" (47).

In light of this consistent scholastic tradition of logical equivocation in the Middle Ages, it is hard to ignore the term *aequivocatio* when it is used in the *Arte de trovar*'s definition of *escarnho,* explicitly marked in that text as being the logical currency of learned "clerigos." The anonymous author of the treatise must have been aware of at least some of these philosophical distinctions when he glossed the *cantiga d'escarnho* as a poetry based on a technique of "palavras cubertas" resembling the learned figure of *aequivocatio:* "E estas palavras chamã os clerigos hequivocatio" (D'Heur, "L'*Art de trouver*" 103). From this definition and gloss, the poetry of *escarnho* emerges as a use of the multiple significations in language for creative (as well as satirical) rather than scholastic purposes.

The modes of equivocal signification and representation underlie the techniques of the CEM's poetry of jokes, with which the poets of *escarnho* create sophisticated games of wit and artifice out of the very figures of equivocal expression, puns (though less common) and plays on words that are considered by Aristotle to be mere accidental products of the imperfections of human language, which inhibit truly logical reasoning. Nevertheless, again according to Maimonides, logic itself may be an equivocal term:

> The term *logos*[,] technically used by the thinkers of ancient
> peoples, is a homonym having three meanings. The first is
> the faculty, peculiar to man, whereby he conceives ideas,

learns the arts, and differentiates between the ugly and the beautiful; it is called the rational faculty. The second is the idea itself which man has conceived; it is called inner speech. The third is the interpretation in language of that which has been impressed on the soul; it is called external speech. (61)

Joan Airas's situation in CEM 180 is an equivocation of the first type, "by chance," since the two Joans seem to have nothing in common but the name. The *mal dizer* of the refrain takes the form of the simplest kind of curse: "the Devil take so-and so!" However, the *cantiga* as a whole is more sophisticated, for the curse does not invoke the demonic name directly, but phrases the curse as a prayer to Nostro Senhor and to Santa María (both vocatives possibly referring to the Virgin Mary, given that the masculine form, in courtly tradition, can be used to address a lady of high station). Joan Airas, the poet, asks the Virgin in a prayer to cause the Devil to perform his work. Joan Airas thus aligns himself with the numinous and proper element of naming and invocation, his namesake with the improper and ominous element. The polarization of higher and nether spheres of cosmic invocation is Joan Airas de Santiago's symbolic mode of distinguishing himself from his homonymous barber. He asks that the latter be "spirited away," since the only means of resolving the equivocation of the proper name involves the total dissolution of his competing double's existence.

The equivocation of names, however, has robbed the curse of its intentional force, as has the mediation of the curse through prayer. A direct curse against the other — "the Devil take Joan Airas!" — simply would not work, because of the dangerous possibility that he himself would be erased. In a curse, there is no way to point out the other except by name; and when the name is equivocal, the curse may fall equally upon the jointly named parties. Joan Airas instead distinguishes between them by using the third-person pronoun, *o*, rather than names, and by filtering the force of the diabolical curse through the mediatrix of divine justice.

The equivocal jokes of the CEM rarely involve puns, in which the form of a word is altered, but usually rely instead on coincidences in form that are built into language without modification. The bad pun usually elicits a groan in the same way that a bad joke or bad dream does; because it takes private pleasure in the manipulation of language that does not communicate intelligibly (Gombrich 105), whereas the *bon mot* and the clever equivocal usage elicit a pleasure that is shared in the communication of a discovery in language itself.

In this light it is interesting to note the list culled by Mário Martins of some of the more telling surnames with obvious equivocal senses from the *Livros de Linhagens*, including: Ladrão ("Thief"), Peido ("Fart"), Caga-na-Rua ("Shit-in-the-street"), Merda-Assada ("Fried-shit"), and so on. It must be noted that these are indeed family names, passed from generation to generation, and hence no doubt the objects of long traditions of onomastic mockery. Carolina Michaëlis insisted on the unusually high percentage of such meaningful and insulting surnames in Portugal (Martins, *A Sátira* 113–116). A few examples will make the undeniable attraction in the CEM for this type of onomastic play evident.

Martin Soárez directs a pair of *cantigas* against an undistinguished member of the low nobility, "escudeiro de pequeno logo," according to CBN's rubric, who has pretensions to knighthood:

> Albardan had a horse and nag,
> and wanted to be a knight;
> When I first found this out
> I was so surprised I couldn't believe it;
> And I was right, since I have never seen made,
> since I was born, a knight from a buffoon ["albardan"].

> [Ouv' Albardan caval' e seendeiro
> e cuidava cavaleiro ser;
> Quand' eu soub' estas novas primeiro
> maravilhei-m'e nono quis creer;
> fiz dereito, ca [eu] non vi fazer
> des que naci, d'albardan cavaleiro.] (CEM 290)

The *cantiga* drives home the *escudeiro*'s unfitness for knighthood by insisting on the oxymoron of social status that it would create, an "albardan cavaleiro." The poor squire, who may have perfectly legitimate social claims to knighthood, has the unfortunate personal name Albardan, which Martin Soárez exploits in its common meaning of "buffoon, joker" to reflect on the unworthiness of the name's bearer. (The word *albardan* itself derives from an Arabic root whose principal meaning is, literally, "coldness.")

The *Siete partidas* (2.21.12) make explicit the criteria that bar eligibility for knighthood, in a chapter that has received some attention on account of Don Quijote's knighting "por escarnio," a procedure that effectively disqualifies him from the orders of chivalry (Cervantes 48–49). The Alfonsine code specifies that a potential knight cannot be unsound in mind, under age, or poor, so that the order itself should not have to suffer the indignity of beggary. Cleanliness is also desirable. The *albardan*, besides the etymological connection mentioned above, was also associated with conditions of poverty and mendicancy, and so, too, the would-be knight Albardan, guilty by association, if only by virtue of his name. This type of equivocation confuses the proper and common name, jokingly and indiscriminately mixing particulars with universals.

What seems merely an unhappy accident of language is turned into a necessary and logical defense of social status in the skilled hands of Martin Soárez, reputedly one of the most adept of all the troubadours (Tavani, *A poesía* 305). CEM 291, also by Martin Soárez against Albardan, is much cruder in its sexual and scatological derision of the targeted *escudeiro*. Here Albardan, fleeing, is said to have been taken in by Orrac' Airas, who sheltered him in a coffer (*arca*). The innuendo may be sexual, as it evidently seems, or scatological, as Lapa considers it. But the poem itself says nothing more than that Albardan did "such a thing" ("atal ren"), as if to imply only that the thing was so unspeakably filthy that it cannot even be pronounced. This contravenes the knightly tenet of cleanliness.

But the more decisive argument for denying Albardan's claim to knighthood remains his name. In this short poem (CEM 290) Martin Soárez pretends to trace back the putative linguistic origins of Albardan's

name, and in so doing to discover his hereditary social nature. To do this
verbally, of course, is to construct an etymology, which here, in the context of an equivocal name, is to assert the truth behind both names and
hereditary claims to social title. The noble Marqués de Santillana makes a
similarly conservative statement against the dead Álvaro de Luna in the
Doctrinal de privados (ca. 1453), saying "Let every man be content to be
like his father, [every] woman, like her mother" ["Todo hombre sea con-
tento / de sser como fue su padre; / la muger, como su madre"] (165).
Martin Soárez makes the same argument, not about the father but, equivocally and absurdly, about the name of the father.

Other personal names are open to attack on the basis of some physical feature or bodily deformity. Martins gives examples of one satirical
category about physical defects, always a subject of personal satire and
ridicule. But two poems by Fernan Páez de Talamancos ridicule "jograr
Saco" as much for the cut of his name as his figure; it is again a case of
seizing on an unhappy coincidence between the equivocal signification
and some apt correspondence or contrast in the object of the insult. Don
Fernan Páez takes jograr Saco to task for his poor or absent abilities as a
musician and for his shapelessness of his figure (along with the near
obligatory sexual innuendo, possibly here combined with the additional
analogy to *bolsa* 'scrotum'):

> "Sack" would be more fitting, and not "jongleur."
> > God save me, but he speaks your name
> > who calls you "Saco" and not "jongleur."

> [mais guisado fora saqu' e jograr non.
> > Vosso nome vos dirá, assi Deus m'ampar,
> > quen vos chamar saco e non [já] jograr.] (CEM 132)

As is frequently the case, it is difficult to know here whether Saco represents a family name, or a nickname that has stuck to this particular musician. Nicknames, or *alcunhas* in Portuguese, are also often used as

sources of ridicule. The term itself derives from the Arabic, *al-kunya,* though the sense does not entirely coincide. Ordinarily speaking, the *kunya* in Arabic is reserved for the name that indicates an individual based on his kinship relations to another as parent or child, for example (Abū Fulān, Umm Fulān, Ibn Fulān, Bint Fulān). The *alcunha* as it is understood in Portuguese corresponds more closely with the Arabic *laqab,* or nickname, which can derive from any apt particularity about a person.

Scholberg groups a number of such satires on the basis of onomastic equivocation (or "equivocation by chance" [Spade 15]) under the heading of "cantigas jocosas": "Another procedure was to play on proper names or nicknames with a range from rampant obscenity to the most delicate literary subtlety" ["Otro procedimiento fue el jugar con nombres propios o apodos con una variedad desde la obscenidad procaz hasta la sutileza literaria más fina"] (61). Despite the jocosity of these joking texts, however, the laughter that they provoke, as Freud points out in the epigraph to this chapter, is nonetheless intended to wound and injure, at least symbolically, that is through words alone, "purely verbal."

The playing about with names has a potential as limitless as that of names and language itself. Just to take one group by way of example, there are *soldadeiras,* or courtesans, given such *alcunhas* as Maria Negra, Maria Grave, Maria Leve, Moeda Velha, Peixota (Menéndez Pidal, *Poesía juglaresca* 31–33, 121–125; Scholberg, 81–88; Ferreira). The variety here is as rich as in the invention of the beloved lady's *senhal* in courtly love lyrics, but where the *senhal* serves to conceal, to point out with a name without publicly identifying any particular person, the mocking *alcunha* serves to reveal something of the body in the name.

One brief poem, according to the rubrics, makes fun of the name of Fernan Roiz Corpo Delgado:

> I am amazed by
> an angry damsel
> and what she said
> to me the other day:

for she told me that she would rather
be badly formed
than have a slender body ["corpo delgado"].

[Dũa donzela ensanhada
soo eu maravilhado
de como foi razoada
[es]contra mi noutro dia:
ca mi disse que queria
seer ante mal talhada
que aver corpo delgado.] (CEM 137)

This simple joke, based on an equivocation on a family name, also brings into play another poetic register. A *cantiga d'amigo* by Martin Codax, set in the voice of a young woman, evokes her slender body dancing in sacred space in Vigo:

> In Vigo in the sanctuary
> I, pretty girl, was dancing:
>> I am in love! (trans. Jensen)

> [En Vigo, [e]no sagrado,
> bailava, corpo delgado:
>> amor ei!] (Jensen 208–209)

CEM 137, which reports a young *donzela's* speech indirectly, not only plays on the proper name of Corpo Delgado, but also by substitution feminizes him with an echo of the *cantiga d'amigo's* erotic language, thereby providing yet another malicious reason for the *donzela's* rejection of his suit. The hybridizing of poetic registers is yet another aspect of the interpretive indeterminacy provoked by the equivocal poetics of *escarnho*.

2

BIRD-SIGNS AND OTHER ALLEGORIES
OF THE FUTURE

Everything is double and that is the sign of the divine
miracle.

[Tout est double et c'est là le signe du miracle divin.]
— Abdelwahab Bouhdiba (15; Eng. 7)

The previous chapter considered a particular type of equivocation, on
names, that produces verbal jokes that create fundamental uncertainties
in interpretation. These uncertainties, and those produced by other
modes of equivocation, lend themselves to a particular style of rhetoric
that deals precisely in speaking about things that are unknown or uncertain. This type of rhetoric, which deals in the unknown, predictions,
prophecy, or foreknowledge of the future, is called by Aristotle deliberative rhetoric, as opposed to forensic (about the past) or epideictic (valua-
tions of the present, praise and blame, the latter of which is represented
by the unequivocal invectives at the extreme pole of *mal dizer*). The uncertain future has its own ambiguous rhetoric of deliberation.

The ambiguity or indeterminacy of what may occur beyond the here-and-now can bring together the contrasting realities and expectations that produce one form of the comic. Freud writes: "The other source of the comic [after 'the comic of situation'], which we find in the transformations of *our own* cathexes, lies in our relations with the future, which we are accustomed to anticipate with our expectant ideas" (*Jokes* 244). When ambiguous potentialities in the future are transposed into equivocal simultaneities in the here-and-now, they are then subject not to deliberative but to epideictic determinations of value, which, in the case of the comic CEM, tend to cheapen rather than to elevate.

In an important contribution to the study of ambiguity in medieval poetry, Jacqueline Cerquiglini connects the rhetorical use of ambiguous figures to the occult practices of divination and magic, as well as to sophistry:

> The term "amphibole," "amphibolie" very often characterizes the speech of soothsayers, augurs and sorcerers. . . . The critique of ambiguity thus joins in a general attack on divinatory practices perceived as a diabolical art. In the same way, one finds the same cluster of words about "sophism," all considered here in relation to the logical arts of lawyers.

> [Le terme *amphibole, amphibolie* caractérise très fréquemment la parole des devins, des augures, des sorciers. . . . La critique de l'ambiguïté s'inscrit alors dans une attaque générale des pratiques divinatoires vues comme art démoniaque. On rencontre de même la famille des mots autour de *sophisme*, tous pensés en liaison avec la logique et l'art des avocats.] (171)

Medieval refutations of divinatory practices — such as those of Alfonso X's *Siete Partidas* (7.23.1), Nicole Oresme's *Livre de divinacions* or Lope de Barrientos's *Tratado de adivinanza* — center precisely on rhetorical ambiguity and imprecision as the logical flaw in divinatory forecasting. As Nicole Oresme writes:

> the words of the diviners are sometimes of double meaning, amphibolic, two-faced, as we see in many histories; and sometimes they are obscure and can be applied to more than one event or person. . . .] (Coopland 94–95)

> [leurs paroles sont aucunefois doubles, amphiboliques, a deux visages, comme on trouve en plusieurs histoires, et aucunefois sont obscures et pueuent estre appliquees a plusieurs effects ou personnes. . . .]

In effect, the rhetoric of ambiguity recapitulates both the hermeneutic and the effective modes of the occult. The interpretive movement of divination — whether by means of the stars, birds, clouds, the palm, cards, sticks, texts, and so on — is predicated on a hidden correspondence between natural surface phenomena and the variable sphere of human action, through a general supernatural order of interpretation that governs them and opens a channel that may invisibly link, for example, the flight of birds to the outcome of a military campaign. Magical power operates along the same channel in reverse direction, manipulating the outcome by intervening at the level of the corresponding symbolic function: icon, amulet, ritual, or word (bibliography in Cardini, Peters; Freud likewise considers augury an example of self-imposing superstition, *Psychopathology* 331).

These types of symbolic intervention correspond to the second mode of equivocation, "by analogy" (also called of the *pros hen* type), in which, for example, a man (*homo*) and the representation of a man (*homo pictus*) are not distinguished. Therefore, the magical operations carried out on the image or name are sympathetically transferred, in an equivocation by analogy, to the very thing or person that is represented. Foucault describes two special properties that characterize analogy as a form of resemblance, "reversibility" and "polyvalency": "[Analogy] can extend, from a single given point, to an endless number of relationships. . . . An analogy may also be turned around upon itself without thereby rendering itself open to dispute" (*The Order of Things* 21–22).

From a rhetorical point of view, the occult and supernatural processes that predict or affect the future pertain to a discourse of deliberation, which is, in the Aristotelian system, a rhetoric of the future. If forensic or judicial oratory concerns matters in the past, and the epideictic rhetoric of praise and blame evaluates the present, the deliberative mode of rhetoric, like the occult, deals in knowing and shaping the future (Aristotle, *Rhetoric* 1, 3; Lausberg, vol. 1, ss. 59–65).

Divination is, moreover, fundamentally allegorical, in that it mediates between the distinct zones of experience and the unknown, investing particular phenomena of the present with general significance for the future (Cardini 225–227). An anonymous fourteenth-century *Compendium rhetorice* draws on the tradition of the pseudo-Ciceronian *Rhetorica ad Herrenium* to define allegory, or in Latin *permutatio,* as "a trope in which one thing is shown in the word and another in the meaning" ["Allegoria (permutatio) tropus quo aliud in verbi et aliud in sentencia demonstratur"] (Murphy 238).

Allegory thus proposes a doubling of interpretive possibilities, in which a concealed sense is superimposed on the apparent sense. In this, however, allegory is not necessarily ambiguous, since it invokes a controlling structure of interpretation to produce meaning from code. The allegorical level of meaning may entirely supplant the literal level, as in the enigma, or the levels may parallel one another without intersecting, as in typology. Allegory does, however, share with ambiguity its divergence from logical discourse, in which what is said verbally corresponds uniquely to what is meant. Logic thus finds itself opposed by the ambiguous uses of both language and the allegorical.

The corpus of the CEM centers upon a "stylistic nucleus" of just such a rhetorical figure of ambiguity, equivocal *escarnho* (Rodríguez, "La cantiga"), and also contains a number of texts that represent divinatory and magical powers. In keeping with the expressed satirical thrust of the CEM, all of them criticize or ridicule such abilities. However, unlike the logical criticisms of ambiguity as a figure of sorcery and sophism that Cerquiglini addresses, these texts exploit just such a rhetoric of double meanings to deflate the magical allegories of the occult. The deliberative rhetoric of the future gives way to the vituperative evaluations, in the present, of *mal dizer;* while the ambiguous figures of *escarnho* contradict the univocal allegories of augury and divination.

To be sure, the CEM are not without allegories of their own. The cleric Martin Moxa (or Moya), along with his other "moral" satires, pro- poses a riddle that takes the form of a dream interpretation. Upon arriv- ing at an unnamed dystopian regime, where flattery and lies have taken the place of loyalty, ability, good sense, and learning (*crerezia*), he has a re- curring ornithological dream that he offers for analysis:

> While I was there, I often dreamed a dream in which I
> saw ... what? — the hoopoe, and then the garganey tear
> away from the hoopoe the crest that it has. Then the gar-
> ganey ... but what can this mean, and how can the hoopoe
> capture the garganey?! Who can unravel this dream?

> [Mentr' ali foi, tal sonh' ôuvi a sonhar,
> muitas vezes; e no sonho vi quen?:
> vi a bubel', e a cerzeta filhar
> aa bubela a cresta que ten;
> e a cerzeta ... o que quer dizer
> en com' a pôd' a bubela prender?!
> Este sonho, quẽ-no pode soltar?] (CEM 281)

The hoopoe (*bubela,* Cast. *abubilla*) is a colorful bird with a crested head (*Upupa epops*), while the garganey (*cerzeta,* Cast. *cerceta*) is a type of duck (*Anas querquedula*). Both the riddle, as its name in Galician-Portuguese indicates (*adevinhanza,* cf. OPr. *devinalh*), and the dream are among the most common of divinatory techniques. The enigma openly calls for an allegorical interpretation of the inexplicable surface phenomenon, a rupture of expected consequences that is pointed up by the fractured syntax. The apocalyptic thrust of the riddle is clearly that "the weak shall be strong"; though the possibilities of other levels of typological exegesis cannot be excluded. Martin Moxa may also be aiming indirectly at the injustices of a contemporary court that he circumspectly leaves unidentified.

Nevertheless, the use of allegory in this text is atypical, on the whole, of the CEM. It belongs, moreover, to a fairly reduced group of compositions that Lapa categorizes, under the Occitanized heading of the "sirventés moral" as a subgenre apart (*Lições* 128–130), characterized by Tavani as exhibiting a general lack of the semantic "polychromatism" and concrete personal allusions that are habitual in the CEM (*A poesía lírica* 231). Tavani specifically includes Martin Moxa's CEM 281 in this group.

The CEM, however, usually deal in birds of a different feather in their critique of the "alegoria d'agoiro" (CEM 77.15–16). Joan Airas de Santiago (mid-thirteeth century), *burgues* according to the rubrics of the manuscripts, directs four *cantigas d'escarnho* against practitioners of *agoiraria* (CEM 77.8), divination by observing the flight of birds, particularly, it seems, of birds of prey and carrion-feeders such as the raven (*corvo*), the crow (*cornelha*), and the eagle (*águia caudal*) (CEM 178, 182, 186–187; Johan Airas de Santiago, nos. LXXII–LXXV). *Cantiga* LXXII (CEM 178) is a general critique of *agùireiros,* something of an exception in a corpus that regularly names or points to particular individuals, even when they are only indicated as types such as "un infançon" or "Don Foan." José Luís Rodríguez's view that this particular *cantiga* satirizes only the practitioners and not the practice of augury is here accurate in a literal sense, though this is not necessarily the case in other *cantigas* (Johan Airas de Santiago, 39). This particular poem may also indicate a generally critical attitude toward divination by birds, which then becomes an instrument used to ridicule other individual targets (in three other of his *cantigas*) who profess to believe uncritically in such signs. Joan Airas mocks the augurs by contrasting their morbid interest in carnivorous birds with his own epicurean preference for the edible varieties:

> Those who claim to see good and evil in birds and who are renowned for divination wish for a raven on the left-hand side when they are going to enter somewhere else. I say otherwise to them: may Jesus Christ not pardon me if I do not prefer a capon to a big scavenging raven.
>
> And whoever claims to be knowledgeable about birds and bird-signs always wishes for a raven on the left-hand side when he sets out to go someplace. But I ask Our Lord that He give me, wherever I should go, a fattened capon for my meal, and that He give the raven to the diviner.
>
> For I know well how to tell birds apart, and I enjoy a fat duckling better than a kite, a vulture, or a *viaraz* [a bird of prey], which can do me neither harm nor good. As for the foolish diviner who says that a raven is worth more than a partridge, may God never let him make a better choice.

> [Os que dizen que veen ben e mal
> nas aves, e d'agoirar preç[o] an,
> queren corvo seestro quando van
> alhur entrar, e digo-lhis eu al:
> 5   que Iesu-Cristo non me perdon,
> se ant'eu non queria un capon
> que ũ [u] gran[de] corvo carnaçal.
>
> E o que diz que é mui sabedor
> d'agoir' e d'aves, quand a[l]gur quer ir,
> 10   quer corvo seestro sempre' ao partir,
> e poren digu'eu a Nostro Senhor

que El[e] me dé, cada u chegar,
capon cevado pera meu jantar,
e dé o corvo ao agoirador.

15   Ca eu sei ben as aves conhocer,
e con patela gorda máis me praz
que con bulhafre, voutre nen viaraz,
que me non pode ben nen mal fazer;
e o agoirador torpe que diz
20   que máis val o corvo que a perdiz,
nunca o Deus leixe melhor escolher.] (LXXII)

The *cantiga*'s playful satire depends on the contrasting semantic fields, around the generic category of *ave*, that are brought together in each strophe in an iterative pattern that Tavani has found to be characteristic of the *cantiga d'escarnho* (*A poesía* 173–198). On one hand, the carrion-feeding raven ("corvo carnaçal"), especially flying from left to right ("seestro"), the *bulhafre*, the *voutre*, and the *viaraz* all belong to the lexicon of divinatory birds; on the other, in contrast, the *capon*, a special delicacy when fattened on grain ("cevado"), *patela gorda*, *perdiz* ("partridge") make up the ingredients of a fine meal ("jantar"). While José Luís Rodríguez is entirely right in observing that, technically speaking, there are no particular *palavras cubertas* in the composition, as the *Arte de trovar* defines the *cantiga d'escarnho*, there is nonetheless another type of *aequivocatio* operating here upon the word *ave*.

What Aristotle defined as synonymy became to the medieval commentators another type of equivocation that Spade has called "equivocation by context"; William of Ockham, for example, counts this as a third mode of equivocation, one that conflates more than one particular into a single name, as in Aristotle's example, that both a man and an ox are considered to be designated under the same name, "animal." The logical counterargument against this third mode of equivocation corresponds precisely to the poetic maneuver that Joan Airas makes with the "aves" in *cantiga* LXXII.

"Ave," like Aristotle's example "animal," denotes a class of beings, which groups together the different species (a biologist would no doubt say genera, but these are only relative hierarchies) listed by Joan Airas: crow, partridge, and so on. The logicians caution against drawing inferences from reciprocation between class and species, which is precisely what happens in this mode of equivocation "by context," Aristotelian "synonymy," or univocal homonymy. Such equivocal inferences lead to fallacious syllogisms of the following type: "Every ass is an animal, but every man is an animal; therefore man is an ass" (Ziolkowski, "The Humour of Logic" 6–9). The fallacy here is of course that the syllogism, in order to equate a man and an ass, must negotiate the abstract zone of "animality," or the "class of beings that are animals." This logical maneuver makes the ass, as species, stand in for the entire class of animals. This sophistical permutation, magical like the art of divination, is also a kind of allegory, in which one thing is said and another meant.

In like manner to the philosopher's logical refutation of the allegories of sophistry, Joan Airas refutes the allegories of birds put forth by the *agoirador*. He does so, however, not by directly exposing the equivocal basis of that fallacy, which correlates the flight of birds with the good or bad outcome of future events ("ben e mal"), but by playing along with the equivocation in the sort of poetic and connotative *reductio ad absurdum* that the term *escarnho* expresses so compactly. The *Donatz proensals* glosses the verb *escarnir* with the Latin *deridere*, a bringing down through laughter (Uc Faidit, lines 1388, 79, 2575).

The repetition of "agoiro" (or "agoirar") in close proximity to "aves" in lines 2 and 9 establishes the reciprocity of these words in the semantic field of divination. The expressions "catar agoiro" and "catar aves" are virtually interchangeable to refer to the interpretive art of the augur. Examples of this usage abound: Carolina Michaëlis notes that Fernan Pires, brother of the troubadour Joan Perez d'Avoin, was reputed to "catar ben agouro" and to "catar aves" (*Cancioneiro da Ajuda* 2: 355). The verb *catar* (from Latin *captare*) marks the receptive movement of divination, which reads the predictive flight of birds, with its rhetoric of deliberation, as a text. The *cantiga* decomposes the class "bird" into various species of birds with distinct associative registers: on one hand, birds of prey and carrion-feeders with the practices of augury, linked especially to military outings, as in the *Cantar de mio Cid* (Menéndez Pidal, vol. 2, 486) or the *Siete Infantes de Lara* (Menéndez Pidal, *Flor* 110); and on the other, game or farm birds associated with the culinary and gastronomic. This puts the allegorical quality of the former in sharp relief to the materiality of the latter, and contrasts the futurity of divination's deliberative rhetoric with the actuality and demonstrative rhetoric of the here-and-now. As the connotative areas of each expand, they produce an "interference of semantic fields," to adopt Tavani's terminology, as well of temporal fields. This interference modulates between two incongruous images: in the first strophe, that of the domestic capon as a bird of augury; in the third, that of the *agoirador* at table, literally "eating crow." The critique of the "alegoria d'agoiro" thus proceeds neither by means of a simple projection of the principles of augury onto the domain of the material, nor by a purely logical or dogmatic counterargument to these. Instead, it works by highlighting the incongruities that emerge from superposing two connotative and rhetorical domains that have been stretched to their limits. That fundamental superposition is made possible by an equivocal denotation, here "ave," a designation of class common to both specific fields. Joan Airas exploits an equivocation "by context," or univocal homonymy, to combine two radically different zones of language and cultural activity.

A similar strategy is adopted in Gil Pérez Conde's *cantiga* about a royal decree that would prohibit the troops from eating hens (*galinhas*) during the frontier wars:

> The King commanded in all frontiers, in towns, and on the roads, that hens may not be eaten in wartime; for he says that the seeresses say that it will mean the loss of the land.

Let councilmen and knights eat cows and calves, but
hens may not be eaten in wartime; for he says that the augurs say that it will mean the loss of the land.

Let them eat fresh pork and hams, kids, salt pork, and
geese, but hens may not be eaten in wartime; for he says that
the diviners say that it will mean the loss of the land.

> [Pôs conta el-Rei en todas fronteiras
> que nen en vilas nen en carreiras
> que non cômian galinhas na guerra;
> ca diz que dizen as veedeiras
> 5   que será perdimento da terra.
>
> A concelhos e a cavaleiros
> mandan comer vacas e carneiros,
> mais non cômian galinhas na guerra;
> ca diz que dizen os agùireiros
> 10   que será perdimento da terra.
>
> Cômian porcos frescos e toucinhos,
> cabritos, cachaç'e ansarinhos,
> mais non cômian galinhas na guerra;
> ca diz que lhi dizen os devinhos
> 15   que será perdimento da terra.] (CEM 154)

The principal target of the *cantiga*'s satire, as Lapa points out, is the cowardice shown by some of the soldiers in the King's ranks. This *cantiga*
likely refers to Alfonso X, given the troubadour's close affiliation with that
monarch and the fact that a mini-cycle of the king's own poems take aim
at the same figure of the *coteife* (Nodar Manso, "El carácter dramático-
narrativo"). In this context, the decree would prohibit eating hens, in
its surface meaning, and, more importantly, behaving like hens, as cow-
ards, under the principle that "one is what one eats." However, there is an

additional level at play in the parallelistic fourth line of each strophe and in the refrain, which concerns again the predictions of the future made, in this instance, by "veedeiras," "agùireiros," and "devinhos," who predict that eating hens will magically and allegorically induce the loss of territory ("será perdimento da terra").

This *cantiga* dissembles its central concern, namely that cowardice on the part of the troops will directly cause the loss of the war and territory, by intercalating it between two distinct areas of connotation, as in Joan Airas's *cantiga*, those of divination and edible fowl. The incongruity between the two here induces an interpretation of the word "galinhas" that leads away from the parallel series of edibles ("vacas e carneiros," "porcos frescos," etc.) and toward its secondary meaning of cowardly. This mode of equivocation "by chance" is also highlighted by the same overlapping and incongruously associative series that occurs in Joan Airas's *cantiga* against augurs.

The material and demonstrative field of comparison is not always gastronomic; the critique of augury also plays with the sexual double entendre. Joan Airas de Santiago directs *cantiga* LXIII (CEM 186) against a certain lady, whose name he withholds, and the unusual form of divination that prevents her from leaving her house to attend Mass during Christmas week ("oitavas de Nadal"). Her *agoiro* takes the form of a crow that circles beside ("a caron") and above her ("sobre si"), crying "qua, ca." At the same time, however, these prepositions of place, along with the libidinous caws (equivocally also meaning "acá," "here," as in another *cantiga*, by Martin Soárez, XVI) insinuate that it is a man, rather than superstition, that keeps her home. Moreover, as José Luis Rodríguez notes, the man can be none other than a priest, whose black habit is likened to a crow's plumage. The *Libro de buen amor* makes the same analogy, with as similar onomatopoeic equivocation (*cras* 'tomorrow'), in which priests are shown as hungry for the wealth of a dying man:

> Though he's not yet dead, they are already saying the Pater Noster — a bad sign! — like crows plucking at the ass's hide: *cras,* tomorrow we'll take him away, for by rights he is ours.

[non es muerto e ya dizen *pater noster* — ¡mal agüero! —
como los cuervos al asno quando le tiran el cuero: *cras, cras*
nos lo levaremos ca nuestro es ya por fuero.] (507b–d)

The play on *cras,* apparently traditional, also occurs in CEM 187. The
equivocal possibilities of interpretation undoubtedly extend sexual overtones to such apparently innocent phrases as "sa missa oir" (or "sarmon,"
lines 4, 7, 8); while the lady's question, "Que sera?" (line 13) represents at
once the fundamental deliberative question asked of divination about the
future — "What will be?" — as well an echo of the erotic longing in the
cantiga d'amigo and the *cantiga d'amor:* "que farei," "what shall I do?",
as found for instance in a pair of *cantigas d'amor* by Martin Soárez
(XIII–XIV), in the latter of which the phrase repeats in nearly every verse
of the final two strophes.

Joan Airas de Santiago's *cantiga* LXXIV (CEM 187) likewise gives a
sexual twist to the ill-omened *corvo,* which the bird-watching Don Pero
Nunez, speaking to his wife, sees "so near to your house" ["tan chegado a
vossa casa"]. *Casa,* in the equivocal registers of the CEM, also signifies the
female sexual organ. Among the many divergent interpretations proposed for the final line, Lapa's ("e diz: — De nout' a crás terrás finado!"),
if correct, would correspond precisely with the Arcipreste's play on "cras"
noted above, as both "tomorrow" and the crow's caw. In both the caw of
crow, as bird of augury, and the meaning "cras" ("tomorrow"), the future
again makes itself present, in the ambiguous uncertainties both of its fi-
nality and its interpretation.

In still another *cantiga* by Joan Airas de Santiago (LXXV, CEM 182), a
passing mention of "maos agoiros" serves to indicate the inauspicious
deal made by the merchant don Beeito in Montpellier, in which he traded
his "merchandias" for damaged hides, or, equivocally, a case of venereal
disease: "se lhi dañaron mui mal os coiros." The loss of his capital ("cadal")
is less due to the bad signs, however, than to the fact that he sold at a loss
("mercou atan mal"). In this case, however, the *agoiros* have less to do
with the practical techniques of divination than with a general sense of

future expectations, here embodied in the expectations of profit from an investment of capital. A similar usage is found in CSM 285, where *agoiro* simply means general expectations: "Mai-la Virgen groriosa, Reynna esperital, / fezo que a el essa noite engannou agoiro . . ." (lines 53–54), though it is also possible that here the *agoiro* simply serves to contrast the miraculous character of the Virgin's intervention.

In the case of the merchant don Beeito, naturally, the expectations take the form of profit realized on an investment of capital. The notion of "ganançia" put forth by the moneylenders in the *Cantar de mio Cid,* for example, represents a very different sort of risk, and expectation, than the *agorero* Cid's; where theirs is based on the loan of capital (insured by collateral, though poorly in this instance), his is based on the entrepreneurial sword and the luck of "buenos agüeros." The merchant depends less on speculative prognostication, and more on the deliberate use of capital for incremental gain.

The critique of augury and magical practices, within the urban environment of the CEM, leads in several directions. Such practices sometimes fall under a generalized critique of superstition as a mark either of rusticity or, conversely, of esoteric craft. Baubeta provides an amply documented discussion of these texts as part of a larger current of "anticlerical satire," and a number of literary analogues have been collected by other scholars (Garrosa Resina; Callcott). The Arcipreste de Hita, for example, despite being himself something of an astrologer, includes divination and augury in the catalog of low vices of his messenger and go-between Don Furon: "era mintroso, bebdo, ladrón e mesturero, / tahur, peleador, goloso, refertero, / reñidor, *adevino,* suzio e *agorero,* / necio e perezoso: tal es mi escudero" (*Libro de buen amor,* 1620, italics mine). The connection between rusticity and superstition is evident in a *cantiga* by Don Fernan Garcia Esgaravunha against Joan Coelho (CEM 130) in the notorious literary scandal of so-called "maids and weavers" ("amas e tecedeiras") (Lapa, *Lições* 140–142; Vieira). The *cantiga* is a mocking *encomium* of the virtues of the *ama* ("maid") to whom Joan

Coelho had dedicated a *cantiga d'amor,* virtues that underline such domestic and decidedly non-courtly competencies as clothesmaking, cooking, cleaning, milking, castrating young "cocks" ("capar galiões," rendering them *capones*), while her husband takes care of the male piglets ("castrar verrões"). The erotic insinuation adds a sexual dimension to the *ama*'s skills (already present in an equivocal sense of *ama* as "brothel-keeper" and *tecedeira* as "prostitute") as well as a veiled warning to Joan Coelho against castration. The *ama* has other skills as well, however:

> All this she does, and she divines well with straws, and casts spells well with the eye and with the stick, and knows many a good charm.

> [Tod'esto faz; e cata ben argueiro
> e escanta ben per olh'e per calheiro
> e sabe muito bõa escantaçon.]

The precise meanings of these terms are not entirely clear, and undoubtedly loaded with equivocal erotic connotations: "catar argueiro" resembles the phrase "catar agoiro" and is probably a kind of divination by straws or *sortilegium;* "escantar per olho" may well be either to cast or to remove the evil eye, though the *olho* is also a multivalent sexual signifier, as Bataille's *Histoire de l'oeil* and CEM 131 (*olho do cuu* 'asshole') testify; while "escantaçon" appears to be a verbal charm. Notable, in any case, is the connection of these practices — along with their erotic overtones — not only to the domestic rather than professional domains of rusticity and the *casero* (a connection documented since late Antiquity [Martín de Braga; Baubeta]) but also to an area of specifically female labor, namely, prostitution. The marked feminine case of "veedeiras" ("seeresses") in Alfonso X's CEM 154 above, stands in sharp contrast to the generic indeterminacy of "agùireiros" and "devinhos." One of the few work alternatives available to women in a professional capacity, as in the case of the *ama,* was that of prostitution. Pero da Ponte's CEM 367 makes this clear:

> Whoever wants to provide his daughter with a skill by which
> to prosper ought to go to Maria Dominga, who will know
> how to show her one . . .

> > [Quen a sa filha quiser dar
> > mester, con que abia guarir,
> > a Maria Doming'á-d'ir,
> > que a saberá mostrar . . .]

The *arte* or *mester* taught by Maria Dominga, *soldadeira* — whose professional *lavor* (line 28) as the title implies (from *soldo,* "salary") — is that of "ben ambrar," an equivocal expression for both walking and sex, considerably more profitable, as Pero da Ponte indicates, than sewing or weaving (*coser, tecer*), though these labors are also laden with equivocal sexual baggage.

The distinction drawn between the traditional practices proper to *rustici,* on one hand, and "arte" or "sabidoria," on the other, is an important one. The latter terms, in the CEM, are usually reserved for practical knowledge acquired through esoteric learning, and especially to magical or sexual arts. Lapa glosses the term *arte* as "ciência diabólica, manha," while *enartado* signifies the opposite, "rude" or "uncultured," in contrast to *sabedor* (CEM 420.15). The "daian de Cález" of CEM 23 thus practices his "arte de foder," which, as the *cantiga* repeatedly emphasizes, he learned from books saved from the Inquisitorial fire, which are specifically called "livros d'artes." With that esoteric and quasi-magical knowledge, "fode per arte e per sen," and he even knows how to "per foder encantar," in a sort of sexual exorcism or cure (Márquez Villanueva, "Las lecturas del deán de Cádiz"). So too, the magical powers of "Paio das malas artes" are invoked to explain this personage's rapid rise to power (CEM 402). Behind the rustic guise of Paio, as Mussons Freixas has shown, lies partly concealed the eminent figure of Pay Pérez Correa, *maestre* of the order of Santiago, whose "cerame de Chartes" is not only the cloth characteristic of that town, but also an emblem of his years of study in that center of learning.

Soldadeiras also practiced more esoteric *artes,* including magical ones, as the case of the celebrated Maria Pérez Balteira attests. Frequently, the term *arteira* is used to describe the craftiness, especially in a sexual sense, of the *soldadeira.* In CEM 331, Pero d'Ambroa recounts a sexual "shooting match," playing on the double sense of the verb *tirar,* in which Maria Balteira is described as "sabedor e arteira" (line 7), in the sense of having acquired knowledge in matters of arms and sex (cf. CEM 193.14, 384.23–24). Vaasco Pérez Pardal complains to Alfonso X that Balteira is cheating all of them "per arte," by withholding her contracted sexual favors (CEM 425).

Balteira, against whom numerous satires are directed in the CEM, is likely the *soldadeira* depicted in CEM 339 by Pero d'Ambroa, Balteira's erstwhile lover (CEM 425). This "dona atan velha [e] sabedor," (9) "velha puta" (17), who is now in love with a student cleric ("escolar" 7, "clérigo" 14, and cf. CEM 315.9), he predicts will earn her living "per alcaiotar," a profession that involves not only procuring, but also various sorts of medical and magical remedies. CEM 1, by Alfonso X, and CEM 188, by Joan Airas de Santiago, both represent Balteira as a force to be reckoned with. In the former, Alfonso represents her as saying: "ca sempre fui temuda e dultada," while Joan Airas comically portrays the "gran medo" that he has of "dona Maria," risking his body and life by entering "ala." Pero Garcia Burgalês, in CEM 376, plays on the verbs "jogar" (playing dice and lovemaking) and "descreer" (disbelief in dice, and in religion) to satirize Balteira:

> Maria Balteira, por que jogades
> os dados, pois a eles descreedes?

Her "disbelief" in dice — disbelief shared, interestingly, by Alfonso X who, in the *Libro de ajedrez,* explains the superiority of chess over dice as a game of *seso* rather than *ventura* (*Antología* 205–206) — does not stifle her desire to "play," however, in the multiple senses of the word. "Descreer," moreover, does not simply connote a disbelief in dice, but disbelief in Christianity, a theme that recurs in a *tenço* between Vaasco Pérez Pardal and Pedr'Amigo de Sevilha (CEM 428). A similar case of dicing and disbelief crops up in CSM 238, in which a gambler (*tafur*) is punished not for gambling but for his sacrilegious "escarnio da Virgen e seu Filho." Playing about with words, sex, and certainty about the future again come together in the equivocal rhetoric of *escarnho.*

Though Balteira may not believe in dice, she appears to do so in the arts of divination, as evidenced by CEM 315 by Pedr'Amigo de Sevilha. The troubadour examines the auguries of her imminent departure by means of her sneezes ("estornudos") and by birds. In the latter case, the bird she reports seeing upon leaving is the *ferivelha,* though the bird itself bears little on Pedr'Amigo's malicious interpretation: "With the *ferivelha,* you can indeed depart, but never return!" ["Ben podedes vós ir / con ferivelha, mais nunca tornades"]. However, the name of this bird allows great possibilities for *escarnho:* feri-velha, returning to a favorite topic of satire against women: the "velha." In effect, Pedr'Amigo de Sevilha represents her credulity and his own disingenuousness as yet another occasion for verbal jokes.

The same poet's *tenço* with Vaasco Pérez Pardal (CEM 428) has been much studied for its possible documentary value. The question that Vaasco Pérez Pardal poses, however, concerns the "poder" that Balteira possesses to excommunicate ("escomungar") and to absolve ("soltar"). The first, responds Pedr'Amigo de Sevilha, she has had since before the time of King Fernando III, while the second she received from a "patriarca, / fi-d'Escalhola," though the power itself comes from Mecca. Again the semantic poles here are religious and erotic: *escomungar* and *soltar* must certainly refer here to specific sexual practices, while the references to the Banū Ašqilūla family of al-Andalus (Harvey 31–37), and more remotely Mecca (as the Muslim counterpart to Rome) surely point to Balteira's presumed renunciation of Christianity. Looking at these hints more closely, the power of excommunication, which she possesses from before the time of Fernando III, would not merely be an indirect way to reveal her age (as Lapa suggests), but would also indicate that the power of excommunication arose before the military conquests carried out by Fernando into Moorish territory. The excommunicating power is thus intimated to be autochthonous, while the power to absolve comes from afar and from a presumed anti-papacy in Mecca, mediated by the important family of the Banū Ašqilūla. Without trying to push further the interpretation of the obscure poem, two points stand out: that part of Balteira's power is both esoteric and imported; and, second, that it is antithetical to the established orders of Christianity. In any case, the seriousness of both is undercut by the sexual double entendre.

Such accusations of esotericism and irreligiousness are stock in trade in the critique of divinatory and magical *artes*. One baron had accused the Cid of believing more in the bird signs than in God (Menéndez Pidal, *Cantar* vol. 2, 486). In the CEM, the critique is directed precisely against the univalence of such allegorical interpretations, as a critique of the *idiot savant*, whether he take the form of the *agorero* priest, the ignorant doctor or charlatan physician, or the astrologer minstrel turned cleric for money.

Meestre Nicolas receives mordant praise from Afonso Eanes de Coton for his many, but ultimately empty, *artes*, among which count the commonplaces and platitudes which he passes off for esoteric knowledge: "e diz das aves [en] como vos direi: / que xas fezo todas Nostro Senhor . . ." (CEM 42). This physician from Montpellier appears to have served as doctor in Alfonso X's court, where he receives a number of satires on account of his incompetence (Torres Fontes; Alvar, "Maestre Nicolás"; Michaëlis, *Cancioneiro da Ajuda* 2: 534–538). In CEM 334, for instance, he converts healthy men into dead ones, in a comic reversal of the Hippocratic ideal.

Martin Vaásquez, a *jograr* turned cleric, and would-be astrologer, receives like treatment in the CEM. The rubrics describe him as follows: "a jongleur named Martin Vaásquez who prided himself on knowing astrology without knowing anything thereof" ["un jograr que avia nome Martin Vaásquez e preçava-se que sabia d'estrolosia e non sabia en nada"]. Astrology is the one art of divination that Alfonso X spares in the *Siete partidas,* but only on the condition that it be practiced by those who know how:

> Divination means the same thing as assuming the power of God in order to find out things which are to come. There are two kinds of divination, the first is, that which is accomplished by the aid of astronomy which is one of the seven liberal arts; and this, according to the law, is not forbidden to be practiced by those who are masters and understand it thoroughly. . . . Others, however, who do not understand it, should not work by means of it, but they should endeavor to study and master the works of learned men.

> [Adevinanza tanto quiere decir como querer tomar poder de Dios para saber las cosas que son por venir. Et son dos maneras de adevinanza: la primera es que la que se face por arte de astronomia, que es una de las siete artes liberales: et esta segunt el fuero de las leyes non es defendido de usar à los que son ende maestros et la entienden verdaderamente . . . mas los otros que non son ende sabidores, non deben obrar por ella, como quier que se puedan trabajar de aprenderla estudiando en los libros de los sabios.] (7.23.1)

Martin Vaásquez is evidently of the other type. The little that he knew of astrology, extracted from a book, convinced him to take the orders, since he saw a profitable church in the stars; but, according to Estêvan da Guarda and Pedro de Portugal, he prophesied badly, because he ended up with a remote and poor parish. Worse still, he could no longer practice his former *mester* as a *jograr,* as it had been forbidden by King Sancho IV

(CEM 122–124, 329). The criticisms against Martin Vaásquez are particular: they are not a critique of astrology or divination in general, but of an empty pretension to knowledge of any form, including astrology and divination. Michel Foucault, like Alfonso X, defends the epistemological validity of these arts: "Divination is not a rival form of knowledge: it is part of the main body of knowledge itself" (*The Order of Things* 32).

Airas Perez Vuitoron's target, in CEM 77, is a certain Don Gómez, *cura*, whose single-minded trust in the predictions of *agoraria* overrides his faith in God and fear of the Devil. His resolute optimism, in the presence of "boas aves," prevails before a series of ever more calamitous eventualities foreseen by Vuitoron. The *cantiga* reveals, like Joan Airas's LXXII, the poet's attitude of skepticism before such univocal convictions, making evident their underlying hypocrisy. These beliefs are compromised in the *escarnho*, an equivocation of contrasting positions that renders such uncritical dogmas simply laughable. This is the allegorizing habit that Vuitoron takes to task generally as the "alegoria d'agoiro" (lines 15–16).

In Vuitoron's poem (CEM 77), the *escarnho* turns on a subtle *aequivocatio*. Don Gómez, who would "rather have ill befall him with good birds than good with other ones" ["con boas aves ante prender mal / ca ben con outras"] (line 3), mistakes the signs of good fortune for its actuality. Still, what are these other ("outras") birds or *aves*? The polarizing references to God and the devil leave open another equivocal version of "ave," namely of prayer to the Virgin, the Ave Maria. The feathered *ave*, which is the prognosticating text of destiny and the future, may be equivocally contrasted to the quintessential intercessor and miraculous mediatrix of the future, who is the Virgin of the Ave Maria. The Marian cult that so preoccupied the thirteenth century and the labor of her great troubadour, Alfonso X, reaches out to the possibility of an active intercessor not only before the numinous terror of celestial judgment, but also before earthly or diabolical terrors, by means of the miracle.

But the CEM never make this equivocation (of the first type, "by chance"), to all appearances so obvious, explicit. Perhaps a corpus that does not leave God or Christ unsatirized still has, after all, a domain that

remains taboo? "A la fé, Deus, se non por vossa madre, / [que é] a mui
bõa Santa Maria, / fezera-vos en pesar . . ." (CEM 164). The well-known
Marian allegories of the "senhor das senhores" as the beloved *dona* of the
"heresy" of courtly love perhaps do not extend as far as her fifteen (or so)
namesakes, registered in the CEM as *soldadeiras*: Dona Maria Pérez Balteira, Maria do Grave, Maria Dominga, Maria Garcia, Maria Genta,
Mari'Aires, Maria Leve, Maria Negra, Mari'Mateu, Marinha Caadoe,
Marinha Crespa, Marinha Foça, Marinha López, Marinha Mejouchi,
Marinha Sabugal . . . (Rodríguez, "A mulher no cancioneiros").

Medieval alchemists did not hesitate to make an allegory (*permutatio*) of Maria in an *aequivocatio* of their own: *maria* was said to represent
the Aristotelian principle of matter, by contrast to "form," polarized into
masculine and feminine genders (Marteau 18). The alchemical transmu-
tation of matter is thus likened to the miraculous transformative power of
the divine Mother. To her, also, the profane and sacred axes of the CEM
and the CSM compose a demonstrative dialectic of *laus* and *vituperatio*,
loor and *maldizer*, as a *cantiga de loor* epitomizes in its alternating refrains:

> Cursed be he who will not praise
> her in whom all bounties are.
> [. . .]
> Blessed be he who will praise
> her in whom all bounties are.
>
> [Maldito seja quen non loará
> a que en si todas bondades á.
> [. . .]
> Bẽeito seja o que loará
> a que en si todas bondades á.] (CSM 290)

The CEM, however, look downward rather than upward. Their critique of magical and divinatory allegories in the future exploits the equivocal and contrastive possibilities between esoteric ephemera and their

material consequences in the here-and-now: birds of augury as food or libidinous clerics, "domestic" magic as a rustic practice like cooking or castrating chickens, magical or religious arts as sexual techniques, astrological forecast as a quest for material gain. The deliberative representation of the future is replaced by the epideictic evaluation of the present. The procedure of burlesque lowering that typifies carnivalesque laughter provides the comic material of the CEM (Tavani, "O cómico e o carnavalesco"), while the various modes of verbal, representational, and synonymous equivocation juxtapose the contrasting elements in a comic situation. Nevertheless, the associative and combinatory rhetoric of humor makes the jokes at once funny and fearful. This equivocal rhetoric of substitution, condensation, and displacement — that so much resembles the dream work's operation upon the unconscious in dreams — is a game of language that threatens to denature the effectiveness of such forward-looking language acts as the curse or prayer. The apparently innocent verbal joke may conceal a joke of a cosmic order. The critique of magical allegories runs perilously close to a critique of miraculous ones, and the sign that "everything is double" can represent either a future of the divine miracle or, though disguised by nervous laughter, an uncertain present of human abandonment.

3

PILGRIMAGE AND PROFIT

For long roads, longer lies.
[De longas vias, mui longas mentiras.]

— CEM 303

The previous chapter explored the rhetorical relationship between the desires to affect what happens in the here-and-now and to know what will occur in the hereafter. The comic abasement produces laughter that can take the place, within a symbolic order, of anxiety about actual outcomes and events. Both this and the following chapter will consider specific moments of *escarnho* as they bear on this relation, which negotiates the apparently contradictory zones of seriousness and play. What is light-heartedly made into a joking or comic situation in the present masks a deep-seated anxiety that concerns the future. Subsequent chapters will deal with what, on the manifest or surface level, are taboo or obscene sexual encounters and how these give shape to a latent fear of the unknown or of unpredictable consequences. This chapter considers a group of poems that deal with pilgrimage, an endeavor that seeks to reach two places at once, one in the physical geography of the pilgrimage, the other in the transmogrified spiritual plane of eschatological bonus or reward. In the antithetical joking world of the CEM, however, the pilgrimage, critiqued and rendered burlesque, loses the earnest connection between journey of the feet and of the soul, but in turn, and by substitution, makes evident the symbolic link between exposing the venal for what it is, in this material world, and the unattainable pursuit of an immaterial perfect world.

The "burlesque" pilgrims of the CEM are nothing like true pilgrims: they either never even leave their homes, or never reach their destinations, or if they do, do so for all the wrong reasons. These burlesque pilgrims travel not toward Santiago on the Jacobean pilgrimage route, but away from it, leaving Spain and usually ending up in France, even when their hypothetical travel plans were supposed to take them to the Holy Land. In the playful satire of the CEM, this matters little, however, since these are as much textual as geographical travels. These poems turn ordinary expectations upside down, all in fun, to provoke laughter with their jokes, which, while remaining "only jokes," expressed only in words, can nevertheless broach in symbolic fashion the deepest-reaching sources of cultural anxiety.

What makes a pilgrimage burlesque, then? If a pilgrimage is defined by its specific destination, toward which the steadfast pilgrim directs his steps heedless of any obstacles that he may encounter, the burlesque pilgrimage is just the opposite: it aimlessly follows the path of least resistance. A burlesque pilgrimage going to Jerusalem may perfectly well end up in Marseille, as happened to one traveller (CEM 284 by Martin Soárez); and a pilgrim to a shrine in France may decide to call off his trip when he has only gone halfway there, without even bothering to cross the Pyrenees (Pero d'Ambroa; CEM 191 by Joan Baveca).

While the religious pilgrimage is ordinarily undertaken as an act of devotion, as penance, for instance, or to fulfill a vow, or to cure a disease, the burlesque pilgrimage is principally a trip of business or pleasure, and preferably a combination of the two, especially if the business is shady. Burlesque pilgrims may include thieves, beggars, merchants, and especially *soldadeiras,* that is, courtesans or prostitutes. One merchant, for example, goes all the way to Montpellier to trade his merchandise, but all he brings back from France, in exchange, are damaged goods and a case of the "mal francés" (CEM 182 by Joan Airas de Santiago).

As every reader of the *Canterbury Tales* knows, the religious pilgrimage presents an ideal occasion for storytelling, as an entertaining way to pass the time. In the burlesque pilgrimage, however, the time for fiction arises upon the return home, when the burlesque pilgrim must invent tall tales of everything that he failed to experience while on the road — or rather, while not on the road. This last point is pivotal in reading the *cantigas d'escarnho*. In their rhetoric of criticism and humor, these poems take apart the narrative fabrications of these burlesque or armchair pilgrims, holding up their many and manifest contradictions for the purpose of ridicule and general laughter.

One of the principal burlesque pilgrims is Pero d'Ambroa. A cycle of some half-dozen *cantigas* satirizes him for his burlesque pilgrimage to Ultramar: CEM 172, 284, 313, 317, 338, 395. According to his friend and rival Pedr'Amigo de Sevilha, Pero d'Ambroa never made the arduous journey to Jerusalem as a *palmeiro* ("palmer"), but instead took the well-travelled *caminho francês* (as it is called in a Galician-Portuguese *pastorela*), though this pilgrim goes in reverse direction, as it were, to Montpellier, where he remains in comfort for the duration of time that a trip to Jerusalem would ordinarily require. The French pilgrimage route is represented as an easier alternative to the overseas voyage to the Holy Land. But Pero d'Ambroa then has the nerve to claim that he has returned from just such a voyage — "Venho d'Ultramar," he says. He invents the news of his trip, the *novas,* though these amount to little more than a few tales about the storms at sea and the passion of Christ, which he reports as if he had been an eyewitness. Pedr'Amigo de Sevilha comments ironically that were he to take such a trip to Ultramar, he too would have to go no farther than Montpellier to learn such self-evident *novas,* and — why even go that far? — he could stay right at home in Burgos to the same effect (CEM 313).

The journey to the Holy Land, of course, can go by a special name: crusade. However, in the indistinct geography of the *cantigas d'escarnho* there seems to be little semantic distinction drawn between the words *romeu* and *pelegrin* or, referring exclusively to the Holy Land, *palmeiro* and *cruzado*. But the equivocal meanings of the word *cruzar* can explain the apparently unconnected images that are evoked — not only here but throughout this burlesque cycle of "crusade" songs (e.g. CEM 172), — which are especially Christ's crucifixion and the storms at sea. *Cruzar* means "to take up of the cross," "to go on a crusade." But it also can mean "to make the sea-crossing," not to mention, as in the case of the sexual crusades undertaken by *soldadeiras,* "to cross-breed." This multivalent conjunction of connotative registers in the verb *cruzar* has been extensively studied in relation to the Arcipreste de Hita's *troba caçurra* "Cruz cruzada" (Márquez Villanueva, "Pan 'pudendum muliebris'" 249–250, 266; Vasvari, "La semiología de la connotación" 304. Burke, "Again *Cruz*, the Baker-Girl"; Molina; Bueno; Menéndez Pidal, *Poesía juglaresca* 161–168; Cano Ballesta, "Los 'cantares caçurros'"; Alonso Hernández; Nodar Manso, "El uso literario de la estructura del signo genital"; Tavani, "O cómico e o carnavalesco"). Moreover, in this context, the multiple meanings suggest that the choice of imagery in these poems comes directly out of the equivocal lexicon, rather than from life experience, and that this imaginary voyage is one that takes place primarily in language. This rhetorical strategy is generally characteristic of the *cantiga d'escarnho,* which always exploits the possibilities of words with double meanings, or equivocals, to produce their jokes.

There have been some ingenious scholarly attempts to set a date to this burlesque cycle of crusade songs about Pero d'Ambroa. Giovanna Marroni connects it with one of the failed crusade expeditions by James I of Aragon around the year 1269. The fleet that set out did not make it to the Holy Land, because the ships were dispersed by storms along the coast of France, an outcome that would correspond nicely to Pero d'Ambroa's situation. There are some problems with this chronology, however, because Pero d'Ambroa appears to have died some eight years before these events, in 1261, though, as in the case of Joan Airas, this may only represent a case of onomastic homonymy. So this episode may still have provided an immediate occasion for the poems directed against Pero d'Ambroa, or at least represents a historical eventuality. But even so this is by no means a sufficient explanation, because there are other cases of burlesque "crusades" that fit the same narrative pattern but not the same historical circumstances.

In any case, it seems a risky business to make historical arguments about events that, after all is said and done, never occurred. These are "events" that are remarkable for their absence. Pero Gómez Barroso points this out in his own *cantiga* about Pero d'Ambroa's fictional crusade. He says:

> Pero d'Ambroa, God forgive me, I did not make fun of you concerning the land across the sea, and this is why: because I could find nothing in it to make fun of, since you never went there . . . and I don't know how to make fun of you over a place where you've never been. . . .

> [Pero d'Ambroa, se Deus mi pardon,
> non vos trobei da terra do Ultramar,
> vedes por quê: ca non achei razon
> por que vos dela podesse trobar,
> pois i non fostes. . . .

> E da terra u non fostes, non sei
> como vos trobe i. . . .] (CEM 395)

Nevertheless, what he says he will not do, make fun of Pero d'Ambroa, is exactly what he manages to do here, in a use of the classical figure of *recusatio*. What is loosely rendered here as "make fun of" is actually the verb *trobar* in the original text. The art of the poet's *escarnho* consists in making something out of nothing. It is saying that the only history behind Pero d'Ambroa's pilgrimage is that he never went.

But what is curious about this case is that history repeats itself, even when the "event" never occurred. Pero d'Ambroa vows to undertake yet another pilgrimage, this time to Santa Maria of Rocadamour in France. But, as Joan Baveca says:

> [H]e ended his pilgrimage just as he ended the pilgrimage of the river Jordan, for then he made it to Montpellier, and now he has passed Roncesvalles and turned around at Roland's pass.

> [e acabou assi sa romaria
> com' acabou a do frume Jordan:
> ca entonce atá Mompilier chegou,
> e ora per Roçavales passou
> e tornou-se do poio de Roldan.] (CEM 191)

Roncesvalles is of course the site of Roland's last stand, still on the southern slope of the Pyrenees. Once again, the would-be pilgrim only made it halfway to his destination.

At issue here are not historical events, but the recurring narrative patterns of fiction: the diverted journey, or the interrupted pilgrimage. These travels take place mainly in the poetic imagination, in language. The proof of this is that these stories are repeated over and over with different protagonists. Martin Soárez directs a *cantiga* against Soeir'Eanes, another fraudulent pilgrim to the Holy Land. With feigned innocence, the *cantiga* begins:

> Although I have never been across the sea, I know the land well through Soeir'Eanes, who has come from there, as I have heard him tell.

> [Pero non fui a Ultramar,
> muito sei eu a terra ben
> per Soeir' Eanes, que en ven,
> segundo lh' eu oí contar.] (CEM 284)

The joke comes in the lesson of inverted geography that Martin Soárez recites, in which he confuses and jumbles the place names of Ultramar with those of the French pilgrimage routes as well as of local Portuguese towns: Jerusalem, Marseille, Santarém, all of which, he says, lie within a day's journey of each other. The same thing happens in a *cantiga* about Paai Rengél and two other pilgrims (CEM 44). In this mock-epic (Nodar Manso, "La parodia"; Vaquero), these three miraculously survive the fierce battles in Ultramar, for a very simple reason, namely, that they never bothered to leave the Peninsula in the first place.

There is a proverb cited in the *cantigas d'escarnho*, a "verv' antigo," that captures very well the critical spirit of the CEM regarding all these tall tales of false pilgrimage: "De longas vias, mui longas mentiras" (CEM 303), meaning something like "the longer the route, the taller the tale." Precisely when the travels are longest and most serious — crusade, pilgrimage, trade routes — the lies become most unbelievable, to meet the genre expectations of the travel narrative.

Another characteristic of the burlesque pilgrimage, when it does involve travel at all, is that it is by no means motivated by religious devotion, but is rather a quest for pleasure and profit. This is what is known as the *romería gallofa,* from a type of food given charitably to pilgrims (Martín Alonso, s.v. "gallofa"), from which the occupation of the picaresque *gallofo* takes its name. The *cantigas d'escarnho* portray many pilgrims as "business travellers" along the pilgrimage routes. There are merchants like Don Beeito, probably from Santiago, who went to Montpellier on a sex tour: he traded his goods for a case of venereal disease. Also on the *caminho,* there lie in wait professional thieves — both those who pose as pilgrims and those who prey on them. Martin Moxa complains that not even pilgrims are safe these days from the bandits who "rouban caminhos," (CEM 277) while Alfonso el Sabio has a poem in which a *romeu* is accused of stealing (CEM 13). Of course, that is a very easy thing to say: "a pilgrim must have taken it!" Yet another pilgrim, perhaps a habitual beggar on the *caminho,* is called a leper, one of the forms of verbal injury about the body (Madero 62–65). He is warned to stay away; otherwise he will risk internment in the *Gafaria*, or leper hospital (CEM 128).

Along with all these marginal characters there were the *soldadeiras*. For Isidore of Seville, the prostitute represents the etymological origin of sin itself: the word *peccator*, "sinner," he says, derives from *pelex*, "prostitute" (vol. 1, 10.228). When Marinha Mejouchi, a *soldadeira*, denies that Pero d'Ambroa ever went to Ultramar, the implication is that she knows this because she accompanied him on the road to Montpellier (CEM 317). Another example is the famous *soldadeira* Maria Pérez "Balteira," who, incidentally, was the lover of Pero d'Ambroa, among others (Alvar, "María Pérez"). She also undertook a pilgrimage to Jerusalem, though, unlike him, she actually seems to have gotten there in the end. Pero da Ponte calls her "our crossed crusader" ["a nossa cruzada"]. He describes how she received a *pardon*, an indulgence, for having completed the pilgrimage. Unfortunately, on her way home, she lost the pardon, because she did not keep her *maeta* — her suitcase or trunk — locked. With clear sexual innuendo Pero da Ponte insinuates that she plied her trade as a prostitute all the way home (CEM 358). Other poets hint that she has become a renegade from Christianity, returning with both a foreign religion and esoteric sexual and magical knowledge. The verb *tornar-se* here can mean both "to turn around" or to convert, as in the word *tornadizo* or "turncoat," "renegade" (Castro 151–152).

The pilgrimage comes to represent the desire for the other, whether in a cultural, theological, or sexual sense. Some of the *cantigas de romaria* (so called by critics, for convenience, on the basis of strictly thematic criteria), for example, invest the pilgrimage with the erotic longing of the *cantiga d'amigo* (Michaëlis, *Cancioneiro da Ajuda* 879–889). In one by Airas Nunez, who was a cleric from Santiago, a young girl looks forward to Sancho IV's pilgrimage to Santiago, which took place in 1286. But she is really waiting to see not the king, but her lover, who is supposed to arrive in the king's retinue. In another *cantiga de romaria* by Ayras Carpancho, the combined reason for making the pilgrimage become clear: "I had the urge one day to make the pilgrimage to Santiago, to pray, and to see my lover there" ["Por fazer romaria, pug'en meu coraçon, / a Santiag', un dia, por fazer oraçon / e por veer meu amigo logu'i"] (no. 13).

In the *cantigas d'escarnho*, by contrast, these delicately erotic overtones are rendered in a burlesque fashion: whether in the caricature of the *soldadeira*, the overly hospitable *abadessa*, or the homosexual. In the equivocal registers of these poems, Ultramar, and everything having to do with the Moor, is frequently used as an oblique reference to homosexuality (Boswell 279). Such is the case, for example, of Álvar Rodríguiz (CEM 101–102, 116–117) and Fernán Díaz (CEM 377), who were both said to have gone "across the sea" (*alen-mar*), and who are both mocked for supposed homosexual practices. These sexual and cultural crossings, like Balteira's, are typical of the CEM's rhetoric of combination that joins several apparently incongruous zones of anxiety into an occasion for laughter.

The burlesque pilgrimage can also take on the sign of cultural difference. Joan Fernández, who is always referred to in the *cantigas d'escarnho* as Joan Fernández "the Moor" ["o mouro"], may have been a convert to Christianity. One poem satirizes him for wanting to go to the Holy Land as a "mouro cruzado," or "mouro pelegrin," a Moorish crusader or pilgrim (again, these terms differ little, at least in these texts) (CEM 230). This seeming contradiction, a crusading Moor, is interpreted as a sure sign of the Apocalypse: "o mund' é torvado," "the world is shaken up." This topsy-turvy world is precisely the world reflected in the carnival hall of mirrors of the *cantigas d'escarnho*. It is also a favorite topic of the moral *sirventés*, from Martin Moxa's apocalyptic visions to the Unknown Troubadour's eloquent renunciation of this world (CEM 429), who asks, expressing the desire and doubt concerning what he might find in the beyond: "Why shouldn't I leave this land, if I might find a better world?" ["Por que me non vou algur esterrar / se poderia melhor mund'achar?"]

The critique of burlesque pilgrims ultimately wends its way back to the same place as the pilgrimage itself: to Santiago, of course. The cleric of Santiago, Airas Nunez, laments the decline of truthfulness in his moral *sirventés* "Since in the world truth has diminished" ["Por que no mundo

mengou a verdade"] (CEM 69). Some disingenuous pilgrims in Santiago —
it is safe to assume that they are burlesque pilgrims — tell him that, if he
is after the truth, he must seek it on another *caminho:* "outro caminho
conven a buscar," they tell him. Others again tell him to look elsewhere for
the truth: "Alhur la buscade." As the poet says, true life is elsewhere. But it
is just this desire — the desire for a truth that is elsewhere — that motivates pilgrimage in the first place. The jokes and laughter of the CEM, in
their critique of the burlesque pilgrimage and of the *romería gallofa,* go
hand in hand with the ascetic's quest for a better world, in his metaphorical pilgrimage of this life.

4

Obscenity and Transgression in an Alfonsine *Cantiga*

The transgression does not deny the taboo
but transcends it and completes it.

[La transgression n'est pas la négation de l'interdit,
mais elle le dépasse et le complète.]
— Georges Bataille (71; Eng. 63)

The critique of the burlesque pilgrimage in the CEM bridges the zones of
the sacred and the profane. It does so, however, with playful mockery that
never really crosses the line of insulting or attacking religious customs or
institutions. When, however, the topic turns from relatively innocent pursuits to crude and unspeakable ones, the profanity, dirty language, and
taboo subjects raise the stakes of such joking, which can no longer pre-
tend to the innocent status of being "only a joke." Obscenity and sex present, in many contexts, favorite topics for the techniques of comic
abasement, but these can also become instruments for exploring more serious issues. The transgressive "experiment" with the obscene takes the

low road toward asking after the epistemological limits of language and existence.

The well-born Marqués de Santillana, in his famous poetic genealogy, the "Proemio e Carta," will dismiss an entire class of poetry as "vain and lascivious things" ["cosas vanas e lasciuas"] (211): "vile are those who, without order, measure, or meter, compose ballads and songs in which people of low and servile class take delight" ["Infimos son aquellos que syn ningund orden, regla nin cuento fazen romances e cantares de que las gentes de baxa e servil condición se alegran"] (214). In the CEM, too, can be found this dim view of popular entertainments, enjoyed by tailors (*alfaiates*), furriers (*peliteiros*), and barbers (*reedores*) (CEM 287). But contrary to Santillana's implicit alignment of low social station, low styles of poetry, and low subject matter, the practitioners of trangressive and obscene literature can be and often are both masters of stylistic refinement and highly placed members of society, as the writings of another Marquis, de Sade, attest.

This chapter presents as a case study a close reading of what has long been considered among the most improper poems in the entire CEM corpus, composed by no less a figure than Alfonso X, king as well as devout poet and architect of the CSM.

The *cantiga d'escarnho e de mal dizer* by Alfonso X el Sabio, "Fui eu poer a mão noutro di- / -a a ũa soldadeira no conon" (CEM 14), has been called one of the most daring and sacrilegious poems of Middle Ages, on account of its parodic mixture of the erotic and the sacred (Scholberg 85). Another scholar has gone so far as to term it "the most repulsive [prayer or utterance] of all literature" ["la [oración] más repulsiva de la literatura universal"] (Filgueira Valverde, *Sobre lírica gallega medieval* 147). I reproduce the text below from Lapa's revised edition (1970), followed by a very rough rendering in English:

> Fui eu poer a mão noutro di-
> -a a ũa soldadeira no conon,
> e disse m'ela: — Tolhede-a, ladron,
> ca non é est' a [sazon de vós mi

5 viltardes, u prende] Nostro Senhor
paixon, mais é-xe de min, pecador,
por muito mal que me lh'eu mereci.

U a voz começastes, entendi
ben que non era de Deus aquel son,
10 ca os pontos del no meu coraçon

se ficaran, de guisa que logu'i
cuidei morrer, e dix' assi: — Senhor,
beeito sejas tu, que sofredor
me fazes deste marteiro par ti!

15 Quisera-m' eu fogir logo dali,
e non vos fora mui[to] sen razon,
con medo de morrer e con al non,
mais non púdi — tan gran coita sofri;
e dixe logu' enton: — Deus, meu Senhor,
20 esta paixon sofro por teu amor,
pola tua, que sofresti por min.

Nunca, dê-lo dia en que eu naci,
fui tan coitado, se Deus me perdon;
e con pavor, aquesta oraçon
25 comecei logo e dixe a Deus assi:
— Fel e azedo bevisti, Senhor,
por min, mais muit' est' aquesto peior
que por ti bevo nen que recebi.

E poren, ai, Jesu Cristo, Senhor,
30 en juizo, quando ante ti for,
nembre-ch' esto que por ti padeci!

[The other day I went to lay a hand on a courtesan's cunt. She said to me: Take that away, thief! This is not the [time to dirty me, during] Our Lord's passion. Let me be, sinner, as undeserving as I have been of him.

When you began to clamor, I understood perfectly that that was no sound from God, for its notes stuck in my heart, so that I thought then that I would die, and spoke thus: — Lord, bless you, who make me suffer this martyrdom on your account!

After that I wanted to depart, which ought not seem injudicious, as I had the fear of death and nothing else, but I could not — so great a trouble did I endure; so then I said: — God, my Lord, I suffer this passion for love of you, for the passion you underwent for me.

Never, since the day I was born, was I so troubled, God pardon me; and with such fright, I began then this prayer to God, saying: — Lord, you drank bile and vinegar for me, but what I now drink for you is much worse than anything I have ever received.

And finally, Lord Jesus Christ, when I am before you in judgment, remember what I have suffered here for you!

(The bracketed text of lines 4–5 represents Lapa's conjectural restitution of a lacuna in the manuscript.)

The textual and interpretive difficulties of the poem have no doubt affected the critical judgments of the poem since Lapa in his 1965 edition of the CEM noted the poem's "extraordinarily daring ideas" ["extraordinário atrevimento de ideias"]. That comment accompanied an edition of the *cantiga* that put nearly the entire poem (lines 3–31) in the voice of the *soldadeira,* a reading contested by Mettman (312–314) and later abandoned by Lapa in his revised 1970 edition. It was a consideration of Lapa's earlier version in the voice of the *soldadeira,* however, that gave occasion to Scholberg's remark, "I do not think that there is any poem that is more daring or sacrilegious" ["no creo que haya poesía más atrevida ni más sacrílega"], echoing two terms from Lapa's notes that were subsequently excised from the revised edition of 1970. In that revised edition, he largely follows Mettman's reading, in which the voice that speaks in the *cantiga* is, after line 8, that of the poet, though Lapa allows the possibility that the *soldadeira's* discourse might extend as far as line 14. Once, however, the poem is placed principally in a male (and in this case regal) voice, the tenor of critical opinions changes subtly. Lapa's "atrevimento" in the 1970 edition, no longer refers to the poem itself, but only to the poet's "forward" solicitation of sex; Martins (*A Sátira* 106–107), for example, shares this less drastic interpretation, preferring to emphasize the aspects of religious parody and ludic or libertine irony that were also pointed to by Lapa. Other scholars, nevertheless, do continue to refer in passing to the Learned King's "atrevidísima" and "sacrílega" *cantiga* or to its "degradado aspecto blasfematorio" (Pena vol. 1, 210; Filgueira Valverde, *Sobre lírica gallega medieval* 146). A prostitute who would compare herself to God can be evidently as shockingly transgressive as Bataille's statement to the opposite effect, that "this God is a whore exactly like all other whores" ["Dieu, néanmoins, est une fille publique, et en tout point pareille aux autres" (269)].

Beyond the critical shifts in voice and gender, the transgressive character of both the poem and Bataille's comparison arises from their rupture of categorical boundaries between experiencing the erotic and the religious. If the transcendent encounter of the *unio mystica* can only be expressed, and even then imperfectly, by means of erotic metaphors, transgression, to the contrary, stretches the limits of language at one and the same time toward the obscene and the divine, through a polysemic stylistics of equivocation. The many references to the sacrilegious intent of the poem take it for granted that a libertine intention takes precedence over a devout one, and thus suppose a lack of religious sincerity on the part of this poet of Santa María. Martins, in a variation of this view, explains the poet's claim that his own suffering surpasses Christ's as clear evidence of irony, rather than sacrilege, though he also accepts the *soldadeira*'s, as well as the poet's, expressed devotional sincerity at face value (*A Sátira* 106). The rather more balanced position of *bifrontisme* is taken by Filgueira Valverde, who, despite his vehement judgment of the poem, remarks on the irreducible ambiguity of the poet-king Alfonso, troubadour of Santa María as well as author of this "repulsive" text, as an eloquent comment on the "paradox of our dualities" ["la paradoja de nuestras dualidades"] (*Sobre lírica gallega medieval* 147). Indeed, many of the "accursed poets of *mal dizer*" ["poetas malditos do mal dizer"] (Campos) were also composers of more conventional love poetry. Francisco Nodar Manso, considering this type of "sacrilegious prayer" a parody of epic and hagiographic poetry, underscores the importance of this literature of "antisocial laughter" ("la risa antisocial") as a subversive literary undercurrent that makes up "one of the vital voices of the Spanish Middle Ages" ["una de las voces vitales de la Edad Media española"] ("La parodia" 156–157, 161). The present chapter will argue that the erotic and the sacred aspects of this *cantiga* do not exclude each other, but rather represent two complementary modes of distinguishing the limits, through the play of transgression and taboo, of what it means to be both a biological and a social creature.

In *Totem and Taboo,* Freud represents the two-headed quality of the taboo (Janus-faced, like the verbal joke itself) through an analogy to the equivocal meaning of the Latin word *sacer,* which like many other such "primitive" words expresses antithetical meanings (Freud, "On the Antithetical Meaning"; Benveniste, "Rémarques"). The taboo imposed by the word *sacer* restricts access both to that which is too holy for apprehension and to that which is too unclean:

> The meaning of "taboo," as we see it, diverges in two contrary directions. To us it means, on the one hand, "sacred," "consecrated," and on the other "uncanny," "dangerous," "for-

bidden," "unclean." The converse of "taboo" in Polynesian is *"noa,"* which means "common" or "generally accessible." Thus "taboo" has about it a sense of something unapproachable, and it is principally expressed in prohibitions and restrictions. Our collocation "holy dread" would often coincide in meaning with "taboo" (18).

A suggestive example of this semantic equivocation is an anecdote reported by Camilo José Cela in which a ten-year-old boy, refusing to try on a pair of pants in front of his sisters, exclaims: "I won't take off my pants because my 'holy thing' will show!" ["No me quito los pantalones porque se me ve lo sagrado"] (s.v. "Lo sagrado," vol. 3, 340). Bataille relates the contradictory senses of taboo to the notion of a limit that becomes perceptible only in the moment of transgression (Grimes 5):

> It is not only the great variety of their subjects but also a certain illogicality that makes it difficult to discuss taboos. Two diametrically opposed views are always possible on any subject. There exists no prohibition that cannot be transgressed. Often the transgression is permitted, often it is even prescribed. (63; Foucault, "Preface" 33–41)

> [Ce qui rend malaisé de parler d'interdit n'est pas seulement la variabilité des objets, mais un caractère illogique. Jamais, à propos du même objet, une proposition opposée n'est impossible. Il n'est pas d'interdit qui ne puisse être transgressé. Souvent la transgression est admise, souvent même elle est prescrite.] (71; Foucault, "Préface" 754–759)

It is therefore hardly surprising that the specific taboo that connects the erotic and the sacred registers in Alfonso's *cantiga* resists precise definition, especially in light of the textual gap of lines 4–5, where the specific prohibition would have occurred. It appears to concern the various levels

of control of prostitution and sexual activity on holy days: rules of abstinence from sex during Lent, a prohibition against prostitution during that
period or against fornication generally, perhaps a pervasive sense of sad-
ness and mourning particular to the observance of Good Friday, possibly
a ritual or superstitious regard for sexual abstinence on that day, and so
forth. Some specific external considerations will serve to shed more light
on just what implied taboos the missing lines may have expressed.

First of all, there were general pronouncements by the church. In theory, of course, prostitution was always prohibited under the sin of fornication, on account of which the prostitute comes to represent, as much
for Saint Isidore as for Bataille, the primordial figure of transgression in
the face of erotic and sacred taboos:

> With prostitution, the prostitute was dedicated to a life of
> transgression. The sacred or forbidden aspect of sexual ac-
> tivity remained apparent in her, for her whole life was dedi-
> cated to violating the taboo. . . . The prostitutes in contact
> with sacred things, in surroundings themselves sacred, had a
> sacredness comparable with that of priests. (133)

> [Dans la prostitution, il y avait consécration de la prostituée
> à la transgression. En elle l'aspect sacré, l'aspect interdit de
> l'activité sexuelle ne cessait pas d'apparaître: sa vie entière
> était vouée à la violation de l'interdit. . . . Les prostituées, en
> contact avec le sacré, en des lieux eux-mêmes consacrés,
> avaient un caractère sacré analogue à celui des prêtres.] (147)

Similarly for Isidore of Seville:

> *Peccator,* "sinner," derives from *pelex,* that is, "prostitute," as
> if it were *pelicator;* this name was used by the ancients only
> to designate this type of transgressor; later the word came to
> refer to all evildoers.

[Peccator a pelice, id est meretrice vocatus, quasi pelicator; quod nomen apud antiquos tantum flagitiosum significabat, postea transiit hoc vocabulum in appellationem omnium iniquorum.] (Vol. 1, 10.228)

The analogy between religious and carnal vocations is revealed anew in the equivocal senses of the word "abbey" (*abadía*), which in the Middle Ages was used to point out not only the convent but also the brothel (Márquez Villanueva, "La buenaventura" 748–749). There is an echo of this duality in Golden Age erotic poetry dealing with nuns (Alzieu et al. 126–128). The brothel "abbess," in many of the urban centers in southern France, rented her *prostibulum publicum* directly from the municipal authorities, hiring the prostitutes and managing their finances according to the regulations provided by the city itself (Rossiaud 4–9; Servais and Laurend 146–147; Otis 88).

One *cantiga d'escarnho* by Afonso Eanes do Coton, a contemporary of Alfonso X, confirms the equivocal senses of the term *abadessa*: "Abbess, I heard it said / that you were very knowledgable / of all good things" ["Abadessa, oí dizer / que érades mui sabedor / de todo ben . . ."] (CEM 37). Lapa takes this locutive literally, imagining that the poet is attacking an "abbess of lax morals" ("uma abadessa de costumes relaxados") in a daring mix of the sacred and the profane. For the editor, this poem, along with CEM 14, shows a sample of the period's libertine sexual and cultural norms. In fact, the poem's entire joke pivots on the equivocation in the word *abadessa* (line 1), in its two homonymous though apparently contradictory meanings. It is thus not a question merely of a libertine sexual ethos, but of a linguistic equivocation that responds to a formal resemblance between the nuns' *claustro* or convent, and the designated space of the municipal prostitutes, who themselves were also called, at least in medieval Dijon, *claustrières* (Rossiaud 7–8n8). In CEM 148, Fernand' Esquio offers another example of the equivocal potential of this term: "A vós, Dona abadessa. . . ." Coton, the poet of CEM 37, unabashedly asks the "abbess" to teach him her secrets in the art of making love, all the while addressing her as the revered and coveted "senhor" ("lord," the habitual masculine form presumably elevating the status of the lady) of the troubadouresque *cantiga d'amor:*

> you who have good understanding
> of fucking and everything good,
> teach me more, my lady,
> how to fuck, for I know not.

> vós que avedes bon sen
> de foder e de todo ben;
> ensinade-me mais, senhor,
> como foda, ca o non sei. (lines 9–12)

Coton's language oscillates parodically from obscenity to piety: "for the love of God" ["por amor de Deus"] (vv. 3–4), "I will recite the *Pater noster*" ["direi *Pater Noster*"] (lines 19–20), this latter prayer also not immune from sexual innuendo (Ziolkowski, "The Erotic Paternoster" 31–34; see also the parodic imitations of the *Pater noster* collected by Ilvonen, nos. 1, 4, 6–9, especially "la patrenostre d'amors" [no. 6]).

It is not a question here of the bookish and esoteric *arte de foder* unearthed by Márquez Villanueva in another Alfonsine *cantiga* (CEM 23) ("Las lecturas del deán de Cádiz"), but rather of the much more practical art "of this occupation of fucking" ["deste mester de foder"] (vv. 16–17), the office exercised by the brothel "abbess" and her charges. It is important to bear in mind the urban professionalism of these sex workers and their business manager, who was recognized as such by the municipal regulators. Jacques Le Goff reproduces a text from the early thirteenth century whose author, Thomas Chobham, though not quite going so far as to defend the prostitute's profession itself, nevertheless attempts to justify her professionalism in plying her trade: "she does evil in being a prostitute, but she does not do evil in receiving the price of her labor, it being admitted that she is a prostitute" (66). Such a "justification by labor," understood by Le Goff to be a new urban mentality towards earned and commercial income, finds its most robust expression in Celestina's apology for the office to which she gave her name: "I live by my trade, as any tradesman from his own, quite honestly" ["Viuo de mi oficio, como cada cual oficial del suyo, muy limpiamente"] (vol. 2, 101). In the same vein, she inquires rhetorically in another passage:

> Should I support myself on the wind? Did I inherit another estate? Have I another house or vineyard? Do you know of any other means of mine besides this craft? Of what shall I eat and drink, from where obtain my clothes and shoes?

> [¿Auíame de mantener del viento? ¿Heredé otra herencia? ¿Tengo otra casa ó viña? ¿Conócesme otra hazienda, más deste oficio? ¿De qué como é beuo? ¿De qué visto é calço?] (vol. 1, 133)

Once recognized as a legitimately professional, or at least mercenary activity, prostitution comes to be controlled no longer by absolute prohibitions, in the manner of Saint Louis's failed edict of 1254 in which the French monarch expelled prostitutes from within the city walls. Instead, an official administration began actively to regulate the working conditions and practices of existing brothels, as in the more temperate edict issued by Louis in 1256 (Servais and Laurend 151–152; Otis 19–24). Leah Lydia Otis writes:

> The global trend of the thirteenth century, represented by the statutes of Avignon and Marseille, as well as by the ordinance of 1256, was toward the development of a positive policy on prostitution and increasing "governmental intervention" in a realm that had previously been left to function on its own. It is this "interventionism" that laid the founda-

tion of the institutionalized prostitution characteristic of the
late Middle Ages. . . . (24)

Official control of prostitution was exercised with special rigor during the Lenten season and during Holy Week. During this period, clearly,
all sexual relations were proscribed, even conjugal ones (Flandrin 20–23,
91–114; Otis 85). Municipalities closed the houses of prostitution, ordered the prostitutes temporarily outside the city walls, and generally im-
peded their trade, particularly during Holy Week, when penitence and
rehabilitation were recommended to prostitutes as well as the community
at large (Otis 85–89; Rossiaud 8, 35, 63–64; for the Peninsular situation,
Márquez Villanueva, *Orígenes* 128; as well the proverbs concerning the
"puta en cuaresma," cited in Grace 379).

Taking into account the fact that Lent was associated above all with
Christ's Passion, in a process of gradual identification with his suffering
("The popular idea of Lent, which prevailed well into the twentieth century,
was that it was a time of prolonged meditation upon the Passion, with special emphasis upon the physical sufferings" ["Lent," *New Catholic Encyclopedia* 8: 634–636 at 635]), it stands to reason that both psychological and
ritual observance of fasting and abstinence would reach their peak on the
very day of Good Friday (Flandrin 94; Lapa 23–24; Martins 106–107). In effect, Rossiaud remarks that even in the fifteenth century, a period in general
much more amenable to municipal prostitution, its traffic was severely cen-
sured during the period of Christ's Passion (64; Márquez Villanueva, *Orígenes* 152–153). Alfonso X's CEM 14 is set on Good Friday, naturally
(". . . Nostro Senhor / paixon," lines 5–6), just on this day of maximum ho-
liness and, therefore, potentially of maximum transgressiveness.

Beyond this, however, it is difficult to be more precise, since the specific expression of the taboo is to be found nowhere in the text itself, only
as it were immanent in the text, or rather concealed within the crucial
lacuna in the text (lines 4–5). One must concur with Mettman's criticism (314) of Lapa's stated editorial policy of restoring the text with

interpolations that are based only on the literary and stylistic "intuition" on the part of the editor. The latter had explained his restorative interpolations in the preface to the first edition (1965), by saying that "they may perhaps serve on occasion as valid exercises of literary and stylistic intuition" ["valem como exercícios de intuição literária e estilística, acaso admissíveis, uma ou outra vez"] (viii). In spite of this criticism, however, Lapa certainly deserves credit in this case for making an editorial interpretation and interpolation that, while not textually ascertainable, tacitly provide two indispensable critical insights.

The first recognizes that the lacuna in the text precisely coincides with the unspoken taboo that connects the *soldadeira*'s refusal of sex and the Passion of Christ. Her specific refusal ("Tolhede-a [mão], ladron," line 3) is predicated on what we may presume to be a negative (*non*) of more general valence, in other words, a type of prohibition ("ca non é est' a . . .", line 4). It is the uncanniness of this unfinished prohibition, which has the markings of a prohibition but no prohibited object, that generalizes the taboo and its "unspeakable" silence. That general silence, the limit of language that is momentarily discerned in the play of taboo and transgression, is for Bataille the peculiar province of the erotic and the divine (67–69, 268–271; Foucault, "Préface"). The act of restoring the textual gap, therefore, is an ambivalent and paradoxical task that is both necessary in order to interpret the poem at all, and at the same time impossible ever to complete, given the irrecuperable state of the text. Just reading a text can sometimes be a form of literary transgression.

The second consequence of Lapa's emendation is to recognize the implicit narrativity of the *cantiga*, an issue that has been raised with regard to other satirical poems by Alfonso (Nodar Manso, "El carácter dramático-narrativo"). The editorial and readerly act of completion admits not only the textual but also the crucial narrative gap of the lacuna. The definite past tense employed by the first-person narrator, along with the imprecise temporality of "noutro dia," affiliates this text with the lyrico-narrative tradition in Galician-Portuguese and Provençal of the *pastorela*, which habitually recounts stories of sexual adventure that take place "noutro dia" (Meneghetti; Álvares and Diogo; Tavani, *A poesía lírica* 217–223; Lesser). This Galician-Portuguese expression, equivalent to the Provençal "l'altrier," is reminiscent as well of the indeterminate times of the Arcipreste de Hita's *cánticas de serrana:* "una mañana," "primer día de semana," "a la madrugada" (Juan Ruiz 959a, 997b, 1022d). Again there is found, between lines 4–5 of CEM 14, an unexplained jump, from that imprecise and iterable time of erotic narrative to the precise but ritually recurring date of the Passion of Christ.

These two crucial aspects surrounding the missing text of lines 4–5, taboo and narrativity, are not unrelated. The connection between the narrative of sexual adventure and the holy date of Good Friday reveals the parodic procedure that underlies the peculiarly transgressive character of the *cantiga.* The latent taboo attempts to delineate sharply sexuality from the devout adoration of Good Friday, while the *cantiga* transgressively mixes them indistinctly in language that is hybrid and equivocal. In the same way the *pastorela,* a narrative of erotic adventure that takes place in an indefinite past time, is blended with the exemplary ritual narrative of Christ's Passion, that recurs yearly according to a precisely articulated Christian calendar. By means of an equivocal lexicon and narrative technique, Alfonso's *cantiga* superimposes an erotic narrative and the sacred narrative reenacted during Holy Week. The result is a "monstrous" hybridization of discursive registers that is characteristic of a certain species of the comic, namely parody:

> [I]n parody two languages are crossed with each other, as
> well as two styles, two linguistic points of view, and in the fi-
> nal analysis two speaking subjects. . . . Thus every parody is
> an intentional dialogized hybrid. Within it, languages and
> styles actively and mutually illuminate one another. (Bakhtin,
> *Dialogic Imagination* 76)

The parodic and mocking *escarnho* resides mainly in the sequence of three prayers ("oraçon" line 24) (lines 12–14, 19–21, 26–31) through which the poet hopes to communicate directly with God, and in which the language of suffering that predominates represents an attempt to bring together God and the poet in the latter's equivocal and obscene "imitation" of Christ: *paixon* (lines 6, 20), *sofrer* and its derivatives (lines 13, 18, 20, 21), *padeci* (line 31), *marteiro* (line 14), *cuidei morrer* and *con medo de morrer* (lines 12, 17), *con pavor* (line 24), *coita* and *coitado* (lines 18, 23), and so forth (on the similar liturgical parody of the adoration of the cross in the *Libro de buen amor,* see Burke, "Again *Cruz,* the Baker-Girl"; Molina; Bueno). This language of suffering can be used to describe the bodily and spiritual agony of Christ in his Passion, the most prominent image during the fasting and abstinence of the Lenten season and Good Friday. However, the same language lends itself equally to evoke the love-sick sufferings of the *coita d'amor,* the languishment from unfulfilled erotic desire, that is such a widely employed figure in the *cantigas d'amor* as well as in courtly love lyric generally, not to mention the theoreticians of the erotic and poetic techniques of troubadouresque *fin'amors,* such as Andreas Capellanus (Jacquart and Thomasset 121–192).

In CEM 14, the framing narrative of the encounter between poet and *soldadeira* triangulates a third discursive register, an obscene one, which is that of the *cazurro* (Menéndez Pidal, *Poesía juglaresca* 161–168; Márquez Villanueva, "Pan 'pudendum muliebris'" 249–250, 266; Cano Ballesta, "Los 'cantares caçurros'"; Alonso Hernández; Nodar Manso, "El uso literario de la estructura del signo genital"; Tavani, "O cómico e o carnavalesco"; Vasvari, "La semiología de la connotación" 304). The very naming of the *conon* already breaks a linguistic taboo:

> The coarse expressions describing the organs, products or acts of sex are degrading in the same way. These words are prohibited. There is a general taboo upon naming those organs. To name them in a shameless manner is a step from transgression to the indifference that puts the most sacred on the same footing as the profane. (Bataille 135)

[Les mots grossiers désignant les organes, les produits ou les actes sexuels introduisent le même affaissement. Ces mots sont *interdits*, il est généralement interdit de nommer ces organes. Les nommer d'une manière éhontée fait passer de la transgression à l'indifférence qui met sur un même pied le profane et le plus sacré.] (149–150)

Already in the polemics about the medieval French *Roman de la Rose*, Jean Gerson had criticized the book's second author, Jean de Meun, for naming the prohibited organs in a sacrilegious way:

He, through his character, names the dishonest body parts and vile and filthy sins with holy and blessed words, as if any such matter could be a divine thing, sacred, and fit to worship, even outside of wedlock and done by violence or deceit.

[Il, en sa persone, nomme les parties deshonnestes du corps et les pechiés ors et villains par paroles saintes et sacrees, ainssy comme toute tele euvre fut chose divine et sacree et a adourer, mesmement hors mariaige et par fraude et violence.] (Hicks 62–63)

The unabashed tongue of Reason in the *Rose* (Lorris and Meun), accustomed to "speak plainly about things . . . without paraphrase" ["parler proprement des choses . . . sans metre gloses"] (lines 7099–7080) pronounces the words "balls" ("coilles") (line 5537) and pokes fun at the euphemistic use of "relics" ["reliques"] (lines 7109–7122).

Alfonso does not hesitate, at the beginning of CEM 14, to name the *soldadeira*'s sexual organ, not only with the vulgar and derogatory term *cono*, but with the added insult of a pejorative augmentative in -*on*, as Mettman notes (314), in a reading subsequently adopted by Lapa, who includes it in the text of the revised edition rather than relegating it to the glossary as a possible manuscript reading, as he had in the first edition of 1965.

What for Bakhtin, in *Rabelais and His World,* constitutes the language of the "material lower bodily stratum," with its carnivalesque levelling of social differences, for Bataille can become, *in extremis,* an obscene language of violence and hatred ("non era de Deus aquel son," line 9), whose existence as a taboo is nevertheless a precondition for the transgressive activity of eroticism toward the divine (138–139 [153–154]). Both writers coincide in affirming that obscenity (to which Bakhtin's "grotesque" gives a more positive twist) involves a principle of continuity between the limits of the body and the outside or another, a momentary interruption of the discrete image of the individual (Bakhtin, *Rabelais* 316–322) or a loss of "self-possession":

> Bodies open out to a state of continuity through secret channels that give us a feeling of obscenity. Obscenity is our name for the uneasiness which upsets the physical state associated with self-possession, the possession of a recognised and stable individuality. (Bataille 17–18)

> [Les corps s'ouvrent à la continuité par ces conduits secrets qui nous donnent le sentiment de l'obscénité. L'obscénité signifie le trouble qui dérange un état des corps conforme à la possession de soi, à la possession de l'individualité durable et affirmée.] (24)

The obscene moment of naming that begins CEM 14, with its augmentative pejorative *conon,* suggests a rupture of the body that is symbolic but nonetheless violent, a linguistic dismemberment in which the organ metonymically comes to represent total identity. Individual "integrity" gives way to the encompassing motive of obscene "dispossession" ["dépossession"]. This is in some ways a formal equivalent to the totalizing force of exemplarity, but of opposite sign. The poet's (phallic) "hand" ["mão"], as well as the "I" ["eu"] of his lyric persona, participates in a process of identification, both sexual and linguistic, that goes beyond the limits of the individual body. Alzieu et al. (343) furnish a number of poetic examples in which the hand becomes a figure of substitution for the phallus; in at least one example (no. 25.19), the sexual connotation of "meter mano" becomes evident, just as it does here in the very first line of CEM 14: "Fui eu poer a mão. . . ." The linguistic contact established between the royal poet's hand and *soldadeira's conon* breaks down, though only for a moment, the social discontinuity of social condition (*estado*) between king and courtesan.

In like fashion, the ritual exemplarity of Good Friday, which proposes a universal imitation, also provides an occasion for a contrary equalizing movement, that of obscenity, whose violence blurs the individual's distinguishing features in an erotic "martyrdom" ["marteiro"] (line 14). The "defacement" of the text itself, in the lacuna of lines 4–5, also forms a kind of obscene continuity, opening the incomplete text to the not entirely recuperable forgetfulness of history (De Man). The crucial, missing textual defect that has created such difficulty in the discursive layout of the poem, blurs the lines that separate the characters of poet and prostitute, their bodies, voices, sexes.

There is yet another aspect of obscenity, in its rupture of the individual's discontinuity, that brings together even more closely this *cantiga's* equivocal registers of the erotic and the sacred. Death, or more precisely the living fear of death, motivates the pursuits of both eroticism and divine eschatology. The poet's obscene "imitation" of the passion of Christ involves not only erotic suffering but also the fear and the intimation of his own mortality (*con pavor, cuidei morrer;* lines 24, 12), even to the point of an obsessive preoccupation with death: "with the fear of death and with nothing else" ("con medo de morrer e con al non," line 17). The spread of meaning of "morrer," of course, may include the topical "to die of love" and simultaneously, in an equivocal register, stand in for orgasm. This latter sense coincides of course with the well-known meaning of the "little death," as Juan Goytisolo writes: "Was not orgasm a little death?" ["¿No era acaso el orgasmo una pequeña muerte?"] (120). Or, according to Bataille: "Pleasure is so close to ruinous waste that we refer to the moment of climax as a 'little death'" (170) ["La volupté est si proche de la dilapidation ruineuse que nous appelons 'petite mort' le moment de son paroxysme"] (189–190; Foucault, "Préface" 764). Similar equivocal usages are also to be found in medieval Spanish literature (Whinnom 373–375; Márquez Villanueva, "El carnaval de Juan Ruiz" 185–186; Vasvari, "The Battle of Flesh and Lent" 10). Alzieu et al. record several examples of similar usages in the Spanish Golden Age (nos. 3.36, 3.43, 83.12, 135.27, 142.23), including this one: "me harás vivir muriendo, / los miembros estremeciendo . . ." (no. 83.12).

The "virtual," connotative, and ambivalent poetics of *escarnho* admits of the paradoxical possibility that the representation of an unfulfilled sexual want can also signify, at the same time, the completion of that same withheld desire (Márquez Villanueva, "La buenaventura de Preciosa" 750–751; Whinnom 373–375; Zumthor 267–281). "Morrer" connotes both sexual privation and release. Both meanings, in the transgressive obscenity of *escarnho,* blend sexuality and death into a vital continuity that marks and goes beyond the taboo limits of being. "Two things are inevitable; we cannot avoid dying nor can we avoid bursting through our barriers, and they are one and the same thing." (Bataille 140) ["Mourir et sortir des limites sont d'ailleurs une même chose"] (155).

The CSM may represent a different mode of reconciliation between eroticism and eschatology, in which the adored Virgin's intercessive "power over life," exercised in her miracles and conditioned by the sublimated sexuality of the Marian cult, mitigates the asperity of God's "right of death" (Foucault, "Droit de mort et pouvoir sur la vie"; Presilla). James F. Burke, for one, has proposed an interpretation of the CSM as a transformative ritual in which the collection's didactic message of love for the Virgin would mitigate and transcend, in yet another form of Marian intercession, the frequent and often unpunished examples of transgression that occur in the narrative *cantigas:*

> He who loved Her might transgress momentarily some aspect of law. But by teaching the love of the Virgin to the

> whole mass of humanity, society as a whole would be trans-
> formed and uplifted so that the deviations of the individual
> devotee would not matter so much. These would not matter
> because it would be made clear, revealed to all individuals,
> that the mercy of the Virgin Mary could evince the state of
> natural justice inherent in the structure of God's universe.
> (Burke, "Virtue and Sin" 251)

Such a new law, principled on divine mercy and mediation, would supplant the retributive justice predicated by an old law of command and
prohibition.

The CEM, however, explore the opposite, prohibited zones of the
Law, testing its controlling retributive force to tolerate or to punish. Eroticism, for Bataille, is the game of transgression that seeks to complete and
transcend the limits of mortality precisely at the moment of the philosophical "death of God" (268–276 [Fr. 296–300]), though this, as Foucault
reminds us, belongs to the realm neither of history nor of logical proof,
but arises out of the philosophical consideration of a sphere of human experience that remains a symbolic one (Baudrillard 240):

> Not that this death should be understood as the end of his
> historical reign or as the finally delivered judgment of his
> nonexistence, but as the now constant space of our experi-
> ence. (Foucault, "Preface" 31–32)

> [Mort qu'il ne faut point entendre comme la fin de son
> règne historique, ni le constat enfin délivré de son inexis-
> tence, mais comme l'espace désormais constant de notre ex-
> périence.] ("Préface" 753)

Alfonso X's CEM 14 toys, by the same token, with the linguistic trans-
gressivity of the obscene, with the same limit of the overriding fear of an-
nihilation. The poet's erotic imitation of Christ's suffering takes place at

the moment of Christ's symbolic "death" as it is annually commemorated and re-enacted on Good Friday. The cyclical time of ritual, however, opens the way for both the resurrection of Christ and the possibility of redemption, in tropological imitation of Christ, for the miming sinner. The narrative that begins with a sexual rejection on Good Friday, in the near past of "noutro dia," ends with a prayer that asks for a vital affirmation of an eschatological order, perhaps prefiguring an "outro dia" in the future. Might not this narrative be imagined to take place, after the manner of the *risus paschalis,* within the general rejoicing of Easter Sunday (Bakhtin, *Rabelais* 78–79)?

This is the profound link, or rather axis of continuity, that the *cazurro* reveals between eroticism, rooted in generation (though it transcends this), and an eschatology that addresses the individual's fear of corruption and death. It is no coincidence that Juan Ruiz's "cantares caçurros" (947b) of the *serranas* immediately follow a death ("Como es natural cosa el nacer e morir, / ovo, por mal pecado, la dueña a fallir . . ." [943ab]; see Lapesa; Walker), nor that they immediately precede the two songs of the passion of Christ, save for a brief *ditado* to Santa María. In that piece that falls midway between the eroticism of the *serranas* and the devotion of the *passiones,* the Arcipreste tells of a prayer he made to God: "e yo, desque salí de todo este roído, / torné rogar a Dios que no m' diesse a olvido" (1043cd).

The Arcipreste's prayer not to be forgotten parallels Alfonso X's to be remembered in judgment ("E poren, ai, Jesu Cristo, Senhor, / en juizo, quando ante ti for, / nembre-ch' esto que por ti padeci!" [lines 29–31]). Both prayers broach the fear of and fascination with the "dispossession" of self, forgetfulness and continuity with the unknown outside. In the obscene limits of language, between the erotic and the sacred, there begins to appear, behind the laughing mask of the *animal risibile,* the terrible anxiety of Rabelais's "grand peut-être" (Lote 39).

5

"Affined to Love the Moor"

Sexual Misalliance and Cultural Mixing

> Uniformity constricts, variety expands.
> [La uniformidad limita, la variedad dilata.]
> — Baltasar Gracián 19

The focus of the preceding chapters has been on issues of religious faith, practice, and doubt and how these can be made the subject of jokes that explore their complexities by bringing them into at times shocking contrast with venal, profane, or obscene matters. Religion, however, is only in part a matter of spirituality, belief, devotional endeavors like pilgrimage or ritual observances, and so forth. In multidenominational communities like those of medieval Spain of the thirteenth and fourteenth centuries, religion also serves as a basic marker of legal, social, and cultural identities. Because these are in themselves potentially fluid and unstable, religious differences may be accentuated in order to govern the rules of association that aim to keep the differences fixed and the communities apart.

In medieval Iberia, the complex interplay of sexuality, language, and culture is nowhere more evident than in this conflictive arena of religious difference. Sexual "misalliances," or illicit sexual relations between members of different faiths, violate both the proprieties of sexual behavior and the limits of what is considered to be acceptable interfaith association. For this reason, two kinds of texts typically permit themselves to speak of such encounters: legal codes, including the *fueros* and the Alfonsine *Siete partidas,* which seek to establish the limits of acceptable social conduct, and transgressive texts, such as the burlesque and satirical CEM, which seek to exceed the same limits. (Marco Antonio de Oliveira Pais has made an extensive study in his doctoral thesis of the inverse relation of the CEM to historical documentation, especially as registered in the law.) The cultural anxiety concerning sexual misalliance has less to do with mere contact than with the concomitant potential for mixing, for losing both self-definition and group belonging. This anxiety asserts itself in the desire to control not only sexuality but language as well. As early as the ninth century, Paulus Alvarus of Córdoba had complained that Christians living under Islamic rule (*mozárabes*) had been seduced by the eloquence of the Arabic tongue (Migne, vol. 121, 555; Sage 28–31; Lévi-Provençal 94–95; Menéndez Pidal, *Orígenes* sec. 87). The recurring preoccupation with mixing — whether sexual, cultural, or linguistic — is apparent in subsequent etymologies of the very term *mozárabe* that stress the notion of mixing between Christians and Arabs. The archbishop of Toledo, Rodrigo Ximénez de Rada (d. 1247), proposes the derivation of the term from *mixti arabi,* while Pedro López de Ayala (d. 1407) furnishes the following definition: "*Mozárabes* means Christians mixed with Arabs" ["Mozárabes quiere decir christianos mezclados con alárabes"] (Glick 193, 343n66; Menéndez Pidal, *Orígenes,* sec. 86n1). Etymologically speaking, the word "mozárabe" derives from the Arabic active participle *musta'rib* 'Arabized'. The tenth verbal form frequently combines factitive and reflexive or middle senses: "to be made . . ." or "to make oneself . . ." (Wright, sec. 61–65).

Language and culture, as such anxious etymologies show, are inextricably bound. Etymology and the history of language can become ways of rewriting and stabilizing determined cultural and political narratives.

Conversely, as Thomas F. Glick argues, "[t]o take linguistic change as a model for cultural change in general is wholly appropriate. The contact of two different languages provides a microcosm of the contact of cultures" (277). The sixteenth-century Spanish humanist Juan de Valdés had made a similar argument as early as 1535, that Arabisms in Castilian indicate novel things introduced by Arabs: "you will find that only for those things that we have taken from the Moors have we no other words by which to name them except the Arabic ones that [the Moors] introduced along with the things themselves" ["halleréis que para solas aquellas cosas, que avemos tomado de los moros, no tenemos otros vocablos con que nombrarlas sino los arávigos que ellos mesmos con las mesmas cosas nos introduxeron"] (30).

While discussing the history of language in pre-Roman Spain, Valdés remarks in passing that warfare and trade are the principal causes of change in language: "The ones who conversed the most in Spain were the Greeks, with arms as well as with commerce, and you already know that these two things are the ones that alter and even change languages" ["griegos fueron los que más platicaron en España, assí con armas como con contrataciones, y ya sabéis que estas dos cosas son las que hazen alterar y aun mudar las lenguas"] (23). A third force, cohabitation, emerges in a later passage that explains the Arabisms that came into the language during the period between the Arab conquest (711) and the Catholic Kings' conquest of Granada (1492) nearly eight centuries later:

> During this interval the Spaniards were not able to preserve the purity of their language enough to prevent a great deal of Arabic from being mixed in with it. Although [the Christian Spaniards] gradually recovered the kingdoms, cities, towns, and places, many Moorish inhabitants still remained there and continued to speak their language until a few years ago, when the Emperor ordered them to become Christians or to leave Spain. By conversing among us they have passed on to us many of their words.

[En este medio tiempo no pudieron tanto conservar los españoles la pureza de su lengua que no se mezclasse con ella
mucho de la aráviga, porque, aunque recobravan los reinos,
las cibdades, villas y lugares, como todavía quedavan en ellos
muchos moros por moradores, quedávanse con su lengua, y
aviendo durado en ella hasta que pocos años ha, el emper-
ador les mandó se tornassen cristianos o se saliessen de Spaña,
conversando entre nosotros annos pegado muchos de sus
vocablos.] (29)

Valdés expresses the process of language change from Latin to Castilian with such quasi-organic terms as mixture (*mezclar*), corruption (*cor-
romper*), and exile (*desterrar,* lit. "to unearth") as well as the word *embaraço.*
This last, meaning "impediment" or "encumbrance," also has the secondary sense of "pregnancy," in keeping with Valdés's naturalizing metaphors
for language change. These concepts of organic continuity and mixing
stand in opposition to the notions of linguistic purity ("la pureza de
su lengua") and the preservation of the original parent language, Latin:
"Despite all these *embaraços* and mixtures, the Latin tongue is still the
principal foundation of Castilian" ["Pero con todos estos embaraços y con
todas estas mezclas, todavía la lengua latina es el principal fundamento de
la castellana"] (30).

Valdés's narrative of language change covers over precisely the particular encounters that make up such a process. The disembodied organic-
ity of language figuratively replaces the live utterances that compose the
complex weave of the social fabric. Cultural contacts, exchanges and mix-
ings, of which language change is a sign, are necessarily polymorphous;
they resist accommodation to ideas of purity (*pureza*), whether config-
ured in terms of language (as Valdés's formulation is) or, alternatively,
sexual conduct, blood, and lineage. Tzvetan Todorov, writing on cultural
mestizaje, argues that what we call culture arises out of encounters with
others recognized to be different: "Identity arises from (the awareness of)

difference; moreover, a culture does not evolve except through contacts: the intercultural is constitutive of the cultural" ["la identidad nace de la (toma de conciencia de la) diferencia; además, una cultura no evoluciona si no es a través de los contactos: lo intercultural es constitutivo de lo cultural"] (22). The normalizing fictions of "pure" culture that shape cultural stereotypes are invented precisely out of resistance to moments of cross-cultural contact, exchange or mixing.

These moments are often figured as sexual pairings. Octavio Paz takes the couple of Spanish conquistador Hernán Cortés and his indigenous lover la Malinche as a foundational myth for Mexican national identity. This identity asserts itself dynamically between the recognition of its heterogeneous origins and the revolutionary desire for rupture with them. As symbolic parents, the "mixed" couple gives rise to a nation constructed out of the violence of conquest and rape, but also out of the productive hybridism of *mestizaje*. Both of these cultural preoccupations are projected onto the sexual relation between Cortés and la Malinche, and find expression in the highly adaptable verb *chingar* 'to fuck', as for example in the exclamation "hijos de la chingada!" (Grimes 76–78). The sexual vocabulary can encompass both the unequivocal violence of taboo language and the complex polysemy of jokes. As Paz puts it, these are words "to whose magical ambiguity we entrust the expression of the most brutal and subtle of our emotions and reactions" ["un grupo de palabras . . . a cuya mágica ambigüedad confiamos la expresión de las más brutales o sutiles de nuestras emociones y reacciones"] (81; Grimes 7).

In the manifold permutations of such equivocal language, conquest, sex, and commerce come together as highly ambiguous modes of cultural exchange. A single word, in the ambivalent contexts of Iberian Reconquest, can open up a constellation of meanings that pertain to different areas of experience. The word *ganancia* 'gain', for example, has a double signification as both conquered booty and financial profit: both the spoils of military victory, and the interest returned on a capital investment. When the Cid, in his capacity as military hero, uses the word *ganancia*, he refers to prospective gains and risks of epic proportions that are very different from those understood by the moneylenders Rachel and Vidas, who finance his expedition (Menéndez Pidal, *Cantar,* vol. 2, s.v. "Ganançia"). The Cid's *ganancia* is made up of whatever he and his troops can win by the force of arms: cities, gold, silver, livestock, clothing, and other forms of wealth (lines 473–481b). For the two moneylenders, by contrast, *ganancia* means specifically the interest due on a loan: "We would relinquish the interest [*ganançia*] were he to repay the principal," they say to Álvar Fáñez after learning of the deception perpetrated against them by the Cid ["soltariemos la ganançia, que nos diesse el cabdal"] (line 1434). Neither of these two senses would seem to have anything to do with sex, were it not for a third expression, *hijo de ganancia,* meaning child born out of wedlock (*Siete partidas* 4.14.1). It may be impossible after all to separate the three senses, since the same word is used equivocally in each case. The "magic ambiguity" of brutal and subtle words can produce such reciprocal representations as, for instance, sexual intimacy as an act of war, or combat as an intimate encounter. Because representations of interfaith sexual misalliances touch on highly taboo zones of both conduct and language, it is not surprising that they often take refuge in equivocal registers, especially those of war and commerce, which are more permissible modes of intercultural association.

All three of these areas of interaction — sex, war, and trade — are drawn together by the operation of the equivocal poetics that characterizes the corpus of CEM. The conquest of Seville in 1248 by Fernando III, "el Santo," marks a decisive point in the complex ethnic relations in medieval Spain that roughly coincides with the reign of Alfonso X beginning in 1252. The event celebrated by Pero da Ponte as the greatest conquest ever "in all three religions" ["en todas tres las leys"], Jewish, Muslim, and Christian (109–111), finds a contemporary echo, but through the eyes of the conquered, in Sālih ar-Rundī's lament on the fall of Seville (Monroe, *Hispano-Arabic Poetry* 332–337).

Ironically, the very success of Christian military endeavors introduced a whole new set of political and social problems concerning the relations and boundaries between the three religions under Christian domain. The enemy so recently overcome had become neighbor, a situation that called for a shift in strategy from promoting hostile attitudes to encouraging, within limits, sociable ones. The regulations concerning life in close proximity attend to the numerous particulars of social and religious cohabitation: living areas, whether shared or separate, the material exchange of goods and services, conversion of religion or political allegiance (Burns, "Renegades"), and last but not least the physical intimacy of bodies, whether lawful or prohibited. Illicit sexual relations between members of different religions present a challenge to the policies of cohabitation advanced by a Christian authority that formally proscribes such relations without being entirely able to prevent them.

Legislation expresses this desire to exert control over life through control over language. A significant part of the Alfonsine cultural project concerned the establishment of universal legal codes: the *Fuero real* and especially the *Siete partidas* (Craddock). The law, as a representation of a social ideal, is precisely the type of monologic discourse that pretends to be completely univocal and to be able to regulate its own signification. The penultimate title of the *Siete partidas* — "Concerning the significance of words and matters which are doubtful" ["Del significamiento de las palabras et de las cosas dubdosas et de las reglas derechas"] (7.33.0) — addresses the problem of ambiguities in language and offers a protocol for resolving conflicting interpretations of the letter of the law:

> The significance and interpretation of words are intended to show and set forth clearly the proper name of the thing concerning which a dispute has arisen. . . . And because, as the learned men of the ancients declared, words and acts of an ambiguous character are, as it were, endless in number and no man can, for this reason, lay down a positive doctrine for every case which may occur; we shall speak of expressions

which are general and common, and by analogy, the meaning of others which occur from time to time, can be determined.

[Significamiento et declaramiento de palabra tanto quiere decir como demostrar et espaladinar claramente el propio nombre de la cosa sobre que es la contienda. . . . Et porque segunt dixeron los sabios antiguos las maneras de las palabras et de los fechos dubdosos son como sin fin, por ende non podrie home poner cierta doctrina sobre cada una de las que podrien acaescer: mas sobre las razones generales que son usadas fablaremos, et segunt la semejanza destas podriense librar las otras que acaescen de nuevo.] (7.33.1)

In a revealing conjunction of temporal and hermeneutic authority, only the king is permitted to interpret the letter of law in cases of doubt: "No one shall interpret or explain the laws except the king, when any doubt arises concerning words or their meaning . . ." ["Espaladinar nin esclarecer non puede ninguno las leyes sinon el rey quando dubda acaesciere sobre las palabras ó el entendimiento dellas . . ."] (7.33.4). The law, which attempts to restrict the infinite ambiguities of language, represents the discursive antithesis of *escarnho* poetry, which thrives on multiplying rather than restricting equivocations and bifurcating senses. Both discourses, of control and of transgression, provide complementary, but not always symmetrical, views of sexual and cultural misalliance.

The *Siete partidas* explicitly prohibit sexual relations between members of different faiths only in certain combinations of gender and religion, specifically in those instances that involve Christian women and Muslim or Jewish men: "What penalty a Jew deserves who has intercourse with a Christian woman" ["Qué pena meresce el judio que yace con cristiana"] (7.24.9); "What penalty a Moor and a Christian woman deserve who have intercourse with one another" ["Qué pena merescen el moro y la cristiana que yoguieren de consuno"] (7.25.10) (Carpenter, *Alfonso X and the Jews,* chap. 14: "Forbidden Unions" (7.24.9). Mark Meyerson cites similar provisions, contained in the thirteenth-century *Furs,* or legal code, of Valencia: "If a Jew or Saraçen is found to have intercourse with a Christian woman, let both him and her be burned" ["Si juheu o serrahi sera trobat que iaga ab cristiana, sien abduy cremats ell e ella"] (88n6). In such cases, the Alfonsine law prescribes death by stoning for the Muslim man, unless the Christian woman is a *muger baldonada,* or public prostitute, in which case the first offense is punished by a public whipping and the second by death. No such distinctions are made in the title on Jews, which simply prescribes the death penalty for the Jewish man in such cases. For the Christian woman, the punishment depends on her civil status. A virgin or widow loses, on the first offense, half her assets, which revert to her parents, grandparents, or to the king; on the second, she faces the loss of all her assets and the death penalty. A married woman is punished at the discretion of her husband, who may have her burned, free her from penalty, or do with her as he likes. Finally, a prostitute faces a public whipping for the first offence, and the death penalty for the second.

But twin double standards seem to apply along the axes of gender and religion. No such prohibitions are articulated for relations involving Christian men and Jewish or Muslim women. Though these too were prohibited under canon law, the ample tolerance for such civil arrangements as concubinage extended in some degree to Christian men's relations with minority women, as legal, historical, literary, and even pictorial documents testify. According to the *Siete partidas,* "the Holy Church forbids Christians to keep concubines, because they live with them in mortal sin. The wise men of the ancients, however, who made the laws, permitted certain persons to keep them without being liable to a temporal penalty . . ." ["Barraganas defiende santa eglesia que non tenga ningunt cristiano, porque viven con ellas en pecado mortal. Pero los antiguos que fecieron las leyes consintieron que algunos las podiesen haber sin pena temporal . . ."] (7.14.0). Yitzhak Baer reports notices of Jewish *barraganas,* or concubines, in Christian Seville (vol. 1, 313n), while Mark D. Meyerson documents the institutionalized prostitution of Muslim women in Valencia. David Nirenberg provides a wealth of historical testimony and commentary on interfaith sexual relations (127–65). In works of literature, the infamous dean of Cádiz, satirized by Alfonso X in CEM 23, indiscriminately includes *mouras* among the many initiates into his esoteric *arte do foder* (Márquez Villanueva, "Las lecturas del deán de Cádiz"). The Arcipreste de Hita pursues an Arabic-speaking *mora* without success, saying that he wants to "marry" her (*casar*) (Juan Ruiz 1508–1512 and note), referring not to the sacrament of matrimony but rather to concubinage or simply sexual union (for this sense of *casar* as sexual union, compare the equivocal usage of CEM 340: "sodes solteiro, e seredes casado"; Roncaglia; Cano Ballesta, "¿Pretende casarse. . . ."), especially given that intermarriage was forbidden without a promise to convert before the consummation of the marriage: "[N]o Christian should marry a Jewess, Moorish woman, a heretic, or any other woman who does not profess the Christian religion" ["[N]ingunt cristiano non debe casar con judia, ni con mora, nin con hereja nin con otra muger que non toviese la ley de los cristianos"] (*Siete partidas* 4.2.15). The illuminations of the Alfonsine *Libro de los juegos* present a direct depiction of the Learned King himself playing chess in the company of two thinly veiled Moorish women (Márquez Villanueva, *El concepto* 272–274).

Whereas these relations enjoy a certain tolerance, the punishments for Christian women and Jewish or Moorish men appear inordinately severe. The law, in prohibiting interfaith sexual misalliances, is concerned with something more than interfaith sexuality alone. It protects the hierarchies of power that maintain the dominance, on one hand, of men over women and, on the other, of Christendom over other religious groups. Both women's sexuality and minority religious affiliations connect in ideologies of the "pure," of confinement and control. The special horror, and consequently the horrible punishments, for sexual misalliance and for renegades from the faith derive less from a fear of difference than from fear of hybridity, mixing, and equivocation. Dwayne E. Carpenter has argued that the *Siete partidas*'s title on Moors serves to discourage conversion from Christianity to Islam ("Alfonso X el Sabio y los moros" 230–232), and elsewhere has noted that "[i]llicit relations between Jewish men and

Christian women do not merely constitute adultery; they represent the linking of believer with unbeliever" (*Alfonso X and the Jews* 92). The *Siete partidas* allow a divorce if one spouse converts to a religion different from that of the other, whether from or into Christianity: "What penalty a Christian of either sex who becomes a Jew, a Moor, or a heretic, deserves" ["Qué pena meresce el cristiano ó la cristiana que son casados, si se tornare alguno dellos judio, ó moro ó herege"] (*Siete partidas* 7.25.6); "For what reasons a separation can be made between man and wife" ["Por qué razones se puede facer el departimiento entre el varon el la muger"] (4.10.2); "For what reasons a party who becomes a Christian can separate from the wife, or husband, to whom he was formerly married according to the rights of his religion" ["Por qué razones el que se face cristiano ó cristiana se puede departir de la muger ó del marido con quien era ante casado segunt su ley"] (4.10.3). The *Furs* of Valencia specifies the same punishment, death by burning, for both sexual misalliances and conversion away from Christianity (Burns, "Renegades" 345; Meyerson 88n6). Inherent in the interfaith sexual encounter is a principle of convertibility and risk taking. Sleeping with the enemy can involve a lapse in one's own religious identity, a kind of apostasy in the flesh; reciprocally, turning away from one's own religion is considered, in the *Siete partidas,* "spiritual adultery" or "spiritual fornication":

> "[A] person who becomes a heretic, a Moor, or a Jew, cannot accuse his wife of adultery, and this is the rule for the reason that he himself committed adultery spiritually" ["[N]on puede acusar de adulterio á su muger el que se tornase herege, ó moro ó judio, et esto es porque fizo adulterio espiritualmiente"] (4.9.8).

> "The same rule applies to a person who commits fornication spiritually, by turning heretic, Moor, or Jew" ["Eso mesmo serie del que feciese fornicio espiritualmiente tornándose herege, ó moro ó judio"] (4.10.2).

The law makes special provision for misalliances involving Christian prostitutes. Unlike the married woman, who is given over to the law of her husband, the prostitute is a public concern whose commerce of sex adds an economic dimension to the convertibility of cash, sex, and intimacy with strangers. In the CEM, the *soldadeira* plays this complex part of mediation and exchange. The very name of her office (also called a *mester de foder* in CEM 37), which has to do with *soldada* 'salary' and *soldo,* a type of coin (Latin *solidus*), establishes the link between sex and money. A poem by Pero d'Ambroa narrates such a transaction of objectified labor in the bluntest possible way: "I asked a woman for her cunt, and she asked me for a hundred *soldos*" ("Pedi eu o cono a ũa molher, / e pediu-m' ela cen soldos enton," CEM 333). The poet, finding this price too high, then asks that the *soldadeira* charge him by the piece ("now you will do better in exchange for my love to make a sale by the piece" ["fazed'ora — e faredes melhor — / uã soldada polo meu amor / a de parte"]), in a grotesque linguistic retailing of the *soldadeira*'s body parts that renders her a commodity, which the poet compares to gold and foodstuffs, rather than a provider of services.

The commercial activity of the *soldadeira* in the CEM can also become mercenary, in the approximation of the *soldadeira* to the *soldado,* or soldier. A recurring narrative in the CEM is that of the *soldadeira* who goes off to "do battle" with the Moors: "moiros guerreiar" (CEM 49). The burlesque frontier romance plays on the equivocal possibilities of martial and sexual struggle between Muslim warrior and Christian woman. In one *cantiga* by Alfonso X, the royal poet tells of the mix-up or struggle, *baralha,* when the *soldadeira* Domingas Eanes engages with a Muslim *genete,* or horseman (CEM 25). The language of blows, lances, and wounds that is proper to the epic battle scene here reveals an erotic subtext that deals with sexual positions, genitalia, and venereal disease. These texts parody the language of Reconquest epics or panegyrics that celebrate military victories over the Moors (Nodar Manso, "La parodia"; Vaquero).

Similarly, in a fragmentary *cantiga* by Afonso Eanes do Coton, a *sol-*

dadeira named Marinha Sabugal wants to bring along an old woman as her companion-at-arms in her war (*guerra*) against the Moors. The satire of the *velha,* or old woman, is a commonplace in the CEM, as it was in Roman satire (Richlin 69). In the CEM, the topic comes up in over a dozen poems: 28, 45, 47–49, 78, 195, 203, 247, 309, 310, 315, 339, 313, 386, 428; as well as more incidentally in CEM 7, 71, 216, 244. The generic character of these satires is witnessed by CEM 48, in which Afonso Eanes do Coton mocks Orraca López on account of her age by having her beg him not to satirize any *velha* at all, for fear that she might be mistaken as the intended target anyway. The poem begins by announcing its genre: "Now I wish to satirize an old woman . . ." ["A ũa velha quis ora trobar . . ."]. In this context, the age of Marinha Sabugal's female companion sharpens the incongruity of the scene by pointing to her unfitness — by virtue of age, sex, and sexual orientation — for a combat against the Moors that is military and sexual: "mais a velha non é doita da guerra." (CEM 49)

The famous Maria Pérez Balteira (Alvar, "María Pérez, Balteira") likewise presents a target for satire on account of her presumed sexual contacts with Moors, although Pero d'Ambroa makes it clear that she has received such "dishonorable" treatment not only from Moors but also from Castilians, Leonese, and from most everyone in the kingdom of Aragon ("dos mais que á no reino d'Aragon," CEM 337). The precise degree of Balteira's relations with Muslims has long been a point of controversy that centers around a *tenço,* or poetic debate, between Vaasco Pérez Pardal and Pedr'Amigo de Sevilha (CEM 428). In this poetic debate, Balteira is said to possess the special and mysterious powers of excommunication (*escomungar*) and absolution (*soltar*), the latter of which she learned from a "fi-d'Escalhola," that is, from a member of the Banū Ašqilūla family of al-Andalus (Harvey 31–37). These apparently spiritual powers are no doubt meant to imply magical powers and, equivocally, specific sexual techniques, both of which "Dona Maria" is elsewhere said to possess in fearful degree (CEM 181). Pedr'Amigo goes further to say that her power to "absolve" comes directly from Mecca: "ben de Meca ven / este poder," "ach'en Meca seu / poder." Balteira is said, moreover, to deny the power that God conceded to the Roman Catholic Church: "o [poder] que Deus en Roma deu / diz Balteira que todo non é ren." This claim that Balteira has explicitly abjured her faith corresponds to a requirement for the *muladí* 'renegade' (from Arabic *muwallad)* to be accepted into Islam, which specifies that would-be converts from Judaism or Christianity, as members of the *ahl al-kitāb* 'people of the book', must explicitly renounce their prior religious affiliation ("Murtadd," *Shorter Encyclopedia of Islam*). The example of Balteira's sexual and religious "conversions" lends credence to the perceived connection mentioned above between the interfaith sexual encounter and apostasy. Whether or not to believe Pedr'Amigo is another matter altogether. Might not Balteira simply be a female representative of the opportunistic group of thirteenth-century "renegades, adventurers and sharp businessmen" documented by Robert I. Burns?

As the *soldadeira*'s equivocal narrative of sexual combat with the Moor begins to blur religious boundaries, it also blurs the boundaries of sexual orientation. Men also participate, sexually and militarily, in these mixed melees. One such is Bernal Fendudo (CEM 188). The unflattering sobriquet is probably attached to the *segrel* Bernal de Bonaval, one of several personalities in the CEM who could have their own personal songbook not only as author (18 songs and 1 *tenço*) but also as target (CEM 17, 76, 87, 194, 357). In this instance, the "split" Bernal fights the Moors under the gender-bending identity of a male virago or man-like woman: Joan Baveca calls him a *dona salvage,* or "wild woman," whose insatiable appetite finally leaves him victor on the sexual battlefield as all the enemy euphemistically "die" in his power, spent by the force of his passive aggression.

The Moorish horseman, the *genete* (from Arabic *Zanātī)* who rides his *alfaraz* (from Arabic *al-faras* 'horse'), is always represented in the CEM as militarily and sexually potent, for example in CEM 21, 25, 60 (see Lourie, chap. 7, 72–75). The longevity of this ambivalent, eroticized image of the Moor is demonstrated by Shakespeare's *Othello.* Iago, though he serves the Moor of Venice, nevertheless says that he is not "affin'd / To love the Moor" (I.i.39–40). The "lascivious Moor," (I.i.126) as Othello is called, is rendered even more alien and more threatening as an erotic figure, and becomes a foil for the construction of Iago's own sense of self-possession. "Were I the Moor," he muses, "I would not be Iago" (I.i.57). Here the difference of persons is made into a difference of kind, as Iago uses his own proper name but refers to Othello only as a member of a class, "the Moor."

If imagining the Moor as "lascivious" highlights his divergence from the norms of Christian society, to imagine him also as homosexual only redoubles this difference. John Boswell has argued that "The regular association of minority sexual preferences with the most dreaded of Europe's enemies inevitably increased popular antipathy toward the minority as well as the Muslims" (Boswell 279). As mentioned above, the bounds of orthodoxy and normality are fixed by coordinates that are both religious and sexual, so that crossing either line violates both orders.

Crossing lines of belief and sexuality in the CEM is frequently mapped onto the journey "Ultramar" or "alen-mar," to the Holy Land. Balteira, called by Pero da Ponte "a nossa cruzada," (CEM 358) is one of these burlesque crusaders. Another is Álvar Rodríguez, whom the rubrics describe as "a squire who travelled to the Holy Land and who used to say that there he had been a Moor" ("un scudeiro que andou aalen-mar e dizia que fora aló mouro," CEM 324). Such conversions of convenience are, naturally, condemned by the *Siete partidas*: "What penalty a Christian deserves who becomes a Moor, even if he subsequently repents and returns to our faith" ["Qué pena meresce el cristiano que se tornare moro, maguer se repienta despues e se torne á la fe"] (7.25.5). Álvar Rodríguez thus presents a favorite target for Estêvan da Guarda, who directs five *cantigas* against him (CEM 100–102, 116–117). In one of them, Álvar Rodríguez says that he wants to return to the Holy Land, where things had gone better for him than they have in his native country ("Ten que lh'ia melhor alen mar / que lhe vai aqui, u naceu e criou; / e por esto diz que se quer tornar," CEM 101). *Tornar-se* means to return, but it also means to convert, to become a *tornadizo* or renegade. Along with this line of attack,

Estêvan da Guarda, on the authority of a certain Master Ali, also details Álvar Rodríguez's sexual involvement with a young Moorish boy of his own household (CEM 116, 117). Here, though the accusations of apostasy and sodomy may both arise from a distant journey across the sea, they are made to converge on Iberian soil, in the specific representation of an illicit sexual cohabitation between a Christian and a Moor.

Like Álvar Rodríguez, Fernan Díaz is said to have crossed over in geography and sexual orientation during his trip to Ultramar. Airas Pérez Vuitoron not only describes Fernan Díaz's desire for a same-sex union ("casamento . . . d'ome"), but also says that no Christian has ever witnessed such a desire to be married: "e por este casamento del, de pran, / d'ome atal coita nunca viu cristão" (CEM 80, Mérida). Here "Christian" means simply anybody, as the parallel verses in the other two strophes suggest: "you never saw anyone with such longing for someone" ["d'ome nunca vós tan gran coita vistes"], "there never existed in the world such longing for someone" ["d'om' atal coita nunca foi no mundo"]. However, the expression "nunca viu cristão" still leaves open the possibility of non-Christian eyes and experiences, especially if these are undertaken outside the realm of Christendom. Pero Garcia Burgalês (CEM 377) chronicles Fernan Díaz's trip to Ultramar in search of a master jeweller able to set a particular gemstone (*olho*), which is a secondary meaning of an equivocal word — *olho* 'eye' — that a more directly transgressive *cantiga de mal dizer* further glosses as *olho do cuu* 'asshole' (CEM 131). Fernan Díaz's Bataillesque "history of the *olho*" would not be complete without sacred parody. Pero da Ponte sings mock praise of Fernan Díaz as a good Christian for never having loved a woman, and never having failed to love (*nen desamou*) a man, high- or lowborn ("nunc'amou molher . . . / nen desamou fidalgo nen vilão"); the joke here lies in the negation of the word *desamar,* meaning to hate or dislike: thus "he never hated" or "he never failed to love," in the sense also employed in CEM 81, 127 (Brea Hernández). Pero da Ponte also says that when Fernan Díaz dies the New Testament verses "Beati oculi" (Luke, 10:23, Matt., 13:16) will be pronounced (CEM 365). The Latin pun on *oculi* and *culi* only amplifies and reconfigures the latent equivocal sense of *olho* as both eye and asshole played on in other *cantigas* (Hernández Serna 289; Scholberg, 108).

The abasing conflation of face and ass is rendered even more clearly in CEM 340, in which Pero d'Armea's ass, *bel cuu,* applied with false eyebrows and cosmetics but missing a nose, is favorably compared to a maiden's face. A perfect visual parallel to this text may be found among the photographs illustrating Georges Bataille's *L'érotisme.* Labelled only as a "tattooed man" ["homme tatoué"], plate XVI [XIX] depicts a man whose ass is tattooed with a pair of eyes and arched eyebrows.

"Moors" are not encountered only on exotic journeys off Iberian shores. Closer to home, they also coexist within the frontiers of Christian territory. Joan Fernández, for example, is referred to in the CEM as "o mouro" though he was not a Muslim, but, according to the rubrics, only appeared Moorish, "semelhava mouro," and likely was a Muslim convert to Christianity (CEM 297). Although the *Siete partidas* define Moors univocally as those who believe in Muḥammad as prophet and messenger of God, and prohibit intolerance against Muslim converts to Christianity, the CEM's poetics of equivocation makes no such provision:

> "The Moors are a people who believe that Mohammed was the Prophet and Messenger of God" ["Moros son una manera de gentes que creen que Mahomat fue profeta et mandadero de Dios"] (*Siete partidas* 7.25.0).

> What punishment those deserve who insult converts ["Qué pena meresce quien deshonrare de dicho ó de fecho á los moros despues que se tornaren cristianos"] (7.25.3).

"Joan Fernández," says one poet of *escarnho,* "a Moor is fucking your wife, just as you fuck her" ("fode-a tal como a fodedes vós"). The meaning is clear: Joan Fernández himself is simultaneously intended as both the adulterous Moor and the newly Christian husband, who has been cuckolded, paradoxically, by none other than his past self (CEM 229). The many allusions to circumcision fuse religious and sexual practice in a constant reminder of his convert status. The "badly-shaped" ("dos mal talhados," CEM 51) Joan Fernández in one *cantiga* wants to do battle against the Moor, to exact revenge by burning, since they had once burned his penis ("mais quer queimar, ca lhi foron queimar / en sa natura já ũa vegada," CEM 408). Another poet repeatedly criticizes the cut of his dress and, by extension, of his penis: ("Joan Fernandes, que mal vos talharon," "vo-la talharon mal," "sodes vós mal talhado," CEM 300).

By the same equivocal logic, two *cantigas* accuse Joan Fernández of harboring a hidden and fugitive Moor or an *anaçado* (CEM 297, 409), equivalent to Castilian *enaciado,* one of the many names for different classes of converts, in both directions, between Christianity and Islam (Castro 151–152). In principle, to shelter a Moor would violate the edicts against cohabitation of Christians with Jews or Muslims: "No Christian, man or woman shall live with a Jew" ["Cómo ningunt cristiano nin cristiana non debe facer vida en casa de judio"] (*Siete partidas* 7.24.8; Carpenter, *Alfonso X and the Jews,* chap. 13: "Social Relations" (7.24.8); the Ordenamiento de Burgos of 1315 likewise prohibits cohabitation of Christians with Jews or Muslims, cited in Cejador y Frauca, vol. 2, st. 1508n). The irony here, however, is that Joan Fernández, even alone, contradicts those edicts by being himself both a Christian and a "Moor," in the multiple equivocal meanings of the term.

The word *anaçado* (inf. *anaçar*) has an unclear etymological derivation. Apparently cognate to the Castilian *enaciado,* it has at least three possible Arabic etyma that have been proposed: *an-nāziʿ* 'renegade', *an-nāziḥ* 'one who is faraway', 'émigré' and *an-nazāha* 'rejoicing', whence Castilian *añacea* (Corominas). *Anaçar,* besides meaning to become a renegade, also means "to stir up", "to mix" (as in cooking), a sense attested as early as 1318 in Mestre Giraldo's treatises on horsemanship and falconry (Michaëlis, "Mestre Giraldo" 250–257). In light of this second meaning, an unattested Latin derivation (*adnateare*) appears in many dictionaries (Corominas s.v. "enaciado"; Machado s.v. "anaçar"), and many additional speculative hypotheses have been advanced. Rodrigo

Fernández Santaella proposed in 1499 a derivation from Latin *initiatus*: "whence they call those who have become Moors *enaziados,* as it were, initiated" ["E de aqui llaman *enaziados* casi iniciados a los que se tornan moros"] (cited in Martín Alonso, s.v. "enaciado"). Leo Spitzer has argued for a derivation from Latin *natio,* which, in the spirit of stirring and mixing up of *anaçar* may perhaps be paired with the also improbable Arabic *an-nās* 'the people' or *anisa* 'to be sociable', which is supported by Martín Alonso. The uncertainty concerning the word's origins, however, should not obscure the characteristic mix of meanings — a convert, and something stirred or mixed up — that lends the word its peculiarity.

This distinctive combination of senses comes up again in an unexpected context, the cosmic satire, or moral *sirventés,* a well-represented theme in the CEM from the austerity of Martin Moxa to the pathos of the Unknown Troubadour (Tavani, *A poesía* 226–232; Scholberg 119–125). The stirring up of people and their mutability in a *cantiga* by Pero Mafaldo echoes the second Psalm almost to the letter: "I see the people move around and around, / and the nations quickly changing their hearts / as to what there is between them" ["Vej'eu as gentes andar revolvendo, / e mudando aginha os corações / do que põen antre si as nações"] (CEM 399; on variant readings of these verses, see Spina 46–47). In the Vulgate the second Psalm reads: "Quare fremuerunt gentes / et populi meditati sunt inania ..." (Gall.); "Quare turbabantur gentes / et tribus meditabuntur inania ..." (Heb.) (*Biblia sacra iuxta vulgatam versionem*); in the King James version: "Why do the heathen rage, and the people imagine a vain thing?"

Similarly, the famous passage from the end of Paulus Alvarus's *Indiculus luminosus* (854), mentioned briefly above, arises in a rhetorical context that is less well known than the passage itself. The acculturation of young *mozárabes* is taken as a sign of an overturned world and the coming of the Antichrist. This apocalyptic vision uses the figure of *adynaton* to express the image of a world upside-down, which Ernst Robert Curtius explains generally as "age's criticism of youth" (98). But Alvarus's criticism is not only of youth, but also of a newly dominant Muslim culture. That Christians should adopt Arabic speech and customs he takes to be a contradiction in terms, an *adynaton,* and the young, culturally mixed *mozárabe* is considered, as the *anaçado* will be centuries later, a microcosm of a disordered world that is itself mixed up and turned about.

This analogy is made explicit in a poem by Joan Soárez Coelho that is best known for its references to two datable historical events, the Emperor Frederick II's struggle with the Roman Papacy and the irruption of the Mongols into Eastern Europe (Mayer 228–271). Carolina Michaëlis sets the poem's date of composition around 1241–1244 (Lapa, CEM 230). Joan Soárez Coelho sees in these events — as in the desire of Joan Fernández, "o mouro," to go on crusade — sure signs of the Antichrist and of the world's imminent end (CEM 230). He imagines such oxymoronic possibilities as the Moor as Christian crusader or pilgrim to Jerusalem ("o mouro cruzado," "o mouro pelegrin") all turning on the play in the verb *tornar-se,* to become or to convert. The world is not only stirred up ("o mund' é torvado") but, like the *anaçado* himself, it is messed up or mixed up ("o mund assi como é mizcrado"). *Mizcrar,* to mix and to calumniate, is the opposite of *puridade* (Castilian *poridat*), meaning both purity and secrecy. Both words have been identified as likely loan translations from Arabic (Castro 174–175).

If "purity" or secrecy consists in being able to keep quiet about a secret, then "mixing" implies going public by speaking out loud. This loudness is one of the distinguishing features of the CEM, which publicly speak ill of others, either directly or in words that are concealed through equivocation. The connection between *mal dizer* and *mizcrar* is made in a *tenço* in which Joan Soárez Coelho suggests to Joan Pérez d'Avoín that he has been duped by a malicious slanderer about a third party: "— Someone has told you that, Joan Pérez, to speak ill [of him] / . . . / but I know well that someone has slandered him / to you, seeking to do him harm, / since he made you believe that" ["— Joan Pérez, por mal dizer / vos foi esso dizer alguen, / . . . / mais ben sei eu que o mizcrou / alguen convosqu'e lhi buscou / mal, pois vos esso fez creer"] (CEM 221). Such speaking evil (*mal dizer*) or public slander (*mizcrar*) is a special kind of transgressive speech and, as such, is specifically prohibited in the *Siete partidas:*

Some men render others infamous and dishonor them not only in speech but also in writing, by making songs or rhymes, or evil statements of those whom they desire to defame. They do this sometimes openly and sometimes secretly. . . .

[Enfaman et deshonran unos á otros non tan solamente por palabra, mas aun por escriptura faciendo cántigas, ó rimas ó dictados malos de los que han sabor de enfamar. Et esto facen á las vegadas paladinamente et á las vegadas encubiertamente. . . .] (7.9.3)

Moreover, slanders composed in writing or in rhymes are singled out as particularly reprehensible, even should the accusations prove true,

because the evil which men say of one another either in writing, or in rhyme, is worse than that which is spoken in any other way by words, because if not lost the remembrance thereof endures forever, but whatever is stated in another way in words is soon forgotten.

[porque el mal que los homes dicen unos á otros por escripto, ó por rimas, es peor que aquel que dicen dotra guisa por palabra, porque dura la remembranza della para siempre si la escriptura non se pierde: mas lo que es dicho dotra guisa por palabras olvidase mas aina.] (7.9.3)

The CEM, as slanderous texts in rhyme and writing, transgress against both secrecy and purity in the way they loudly mix language, sexualities, and other forms of impure cultural exchanges.

In a *cantiga* by Joan Baveca (CEM 189), a *soldadeira* named Maior Garcia, in order to clear her debts, carries out sexual and economic transactions (*baratar*) with a Christian squire, a Jew, and a Muslim, all in the same day. This same Maior Garcia is mentioned in several other *cantigas* as the lover of various members of the clergy, including a dean and archdeacon (CEM 190, 323, 335). In CEM 29, Alfonso X says that he will "repossess" the concubine (*cadela,* lit. "female dog") of a dean — probably the promiscuous dean of Cádiz in CEM 23 — as collateral for a dog of his that the dean has taken: "Penhoremos o daian / na cadela, polo can." The object of this humiliating transaction, the dean's concubine referred to as "a maior," is in all likelihood none other than Maior Garcia (Mettman 317–318). In CEM 189, Maior Garcia is herself the debtor upon whom her creditor, a Christian squire, wishes in like fashion to take his due ("tomar penhor"). She promises to repay him in turn with what she gains from her business with a Jew and a Moor. The entire poem is full of sexual and economic double entendre. When the Moor agrees to advance funds to her, he will only accept a promissory note, in order to secure the loan, that he is permitted to write over her ("o mouro log'a carta notou / sobr'ela"). This is a grammatical construction that has clear sexual connotations throughout the CEM (as elsewhere "deitar sobre si," CEM 323). The combined transactions of writing and sex produce a *tralado* 'receipt', a copy or reproduction both of the financial contract and of the Moor himself, that is, a child.

What is the significance of this equivocal child, born of the mixed encounters between a Christian squire, a Jew, a Moor, and a prostitute? The *Siete partidas* offer a hybrid etymology for the word *barragana* 'concubine', which would derive from the union of the Arabic *barran* 'outside', and the Romance *gana* or *ganancia* 'gain', in the multiple senses of the word. Even her child is called a *fijo de ganancia,* in a grammatical construction that is reminiscent of the Arabic language in general (Castro 178–181), as well as of the expression *walad al-zinā'*, "illegitimate child," "son of adultery or prostitution":

> The name *barragana* is derived from two words; one of
> them Arabic, which means outside, and the other Castilian,
> which means to gain, and these two words, when united,

mean something earned outside the rules of the church. For this reason those who are born of women of this kind are called children of gain [*fijos de ganancia*].

[["Barragana"] tomó este nombre de dos palabras, de barra que es de arábigo, que quiere decir tanto como fuera, et gana que es de ladino, que es por ganancia; et estas dos palabras ayuntadas en uno, quieren tanto decir como ganancia que es fecha fuera de mandamiento de eglesia; et por ende los que nascen de tales mugeres son llamados fijos de ganancia.] (4.14.1)

The etymology of the word *barragana* is as mixed as the *barragana*'s child, whose uncertain parents are of different stations and possibly of different faiths. The *fijo de ganancia* stands to inherit an ambivalent cultural legacy of conquest, surplus value, and illegitimacy. Maior Garcia's equivocal *tralado* is a bastard text that, like the CEM themselves, records the profoundly ambiguous realities of cultural mixing in medieval Iberia.

6

"Aquí no Valen Dotores"

Christian Doctors and Charlatans

> Doctors mean nothing here,
> only experience counts.
> Here the know-it-all
> Would discover his ignorance.
>
> [Aquí no valen dotores,
> Sólo vale la esperiencia
> aquí verían su inocencia
> esos que todo lo saben.]
>
> — Martín Fierro

The *soldadeira*'s intercultural exchange of sex for money is but one mode of exchange conversion in the newly expanded urban economies of late thirteenth-century Spain. The equivalencies in value that govern a money economy allow a coin, as signifier, to be as if by magical or metaphorical tranformation (*permutatio*) converted into any of a number of other substances (Shell 1–4). In the literary economy of the CEM, however, these equivalencies are equivocally convertible at the level of the signifier, opening the way for fraudulent practitioners of language and signification to change their manipulations of words into manipulations of people and things. Equivocal coinage and ambiguous commercial contracts undermine the very principle of convertible exchange that roots the system of urban professionalism based on equivalencies of specialized services.

The CEM, based on just such destabilizing multiplicities of signification, thus issue a double challenge to the increasingly specialized professionalism that flourishes in the thirteenth century. They question, on one hand, the credentials of practicing professionals, whether lawyers, medical doctors, judges, tax collectors (*talhadores*); while, on the other, imputing a crass desire for material enrichment on the part of these practitioners. However, it seems that the CEM's criticisms of doctors and lawyers are not directed at these newly formed groups of trained, urban professionals as a whole, but instead, given these poems' penchant for particular rather than categorical targets, that they take aim at the worst members of these professions. Criticizing the charlatans, frauds, and most mercenary practitioners of the profession could also be construed as a general apology for these professions. "Look at these bad apples," they would be saying, leaving an imagined audience to then understand, "but the good doctors and lawyers are not so; to the contrary, they are valuable members of society." The critique of charlatans does not necessarily impugn the professional classes as such, because exposing the impostors leaves those remaining unscathed all the more reputable. It is not the doctors of medicine and law per se who are under attack here, but those who see these careers or disguises as merely a means of personal and professional advancement that in no way corresponds to real professional merits: the talents of healing or rendering justice.

If the critique put forward by the CEM is not simply a categorical indictment of professional groups through the use of stereotypes, but rather a critique of self-seeking hypocrites, charlatans, profiteers, posers, *arrivistes,* and confidence men who masquerade as reputable professionals, then these texts call for an interpretation that goes beyond the simple thematic clustering of "caricatures" or "satires of professions" that has guided many approaches to the CEM (Aguiar 64–89; Martins 84–88; Lopes 272–276). The joke made by Estêvan da Guarda about a deaf judge who will not "hear" the plaintiff poet's pending lawsuit (CEM 105) by no means reflects on the legal profession as a whole, since the *cantiga* offers an exact parallel to what the written law itself states about judges. The *Siete partidas* specify that deafness is an automatic disqualification in a judge (3.3.4), offering yet another level of meaning to the multivalent adjective applied to this "blocked" judge ("embargado"). Other jokes about the legal profession include a lawyer so adept in dialectic that he can cure a man from death with it (though, alas, only in legal, not medical terms) (CEM 86). Another lawyer, missing a foot, limps both physically and in his legal reasoning, crookedly (CEM 103). Johan Airas de Santiago sexualizes the law when he invokes the Livro de León as his legal authority for arguing that the woman who has "killed" him (with sexual desire) should be placed "under him" (CEM 185). The joking dialogue of the *tenço* allows Vaasco Gil to come very near to calling, humorously, King Alfonso X a thief or at least a magician ("trajeitador"), apparently for returning a borrowed cape in a condition different (and improved) from that in which it was lent. But Alfonso, legist as well as poet and learned king, also knows the law, responding to the accusation:

> — Don Vaasco, I was once a young scholar
> and used to study Law;
> and in the schools I used to attend
> I learned from the masters the following lesson:
> never to take the coat of another,
> but if I improve it, I do a good thing,
> and therefore am not a thief.

> [— Don Vaasco, eu fui já clerizon
> e Degreda soía estudiar;
> e nas escolas, u soía entrar,
> dos maestres aprendi tal liçon:

que manto doutren non filhe per ren,

mais se m' eu o melhoro, faço ben,

e non sõo, por aquesto, ladron.] (CEM 422)

Another place where the complex interpretation of signs (*catar*) determines actions that result in very real effects on particular individuals lies in the flourishing field of medical diagnosis and treatment. The latter half of the thirteenth century experienced an explosion in demand for medical lore, much of it translated from Arabic sources, as well as for medical services. This also opened the door to a flourishing trade in quackery and medical chicanery.

Luis García Ballester and other historians of medicine and society have documented the preponderance of medical professionals in medieval Spain who belonged to internal minority or marginal communities. The practice of medicine before the times of expulsion and inquisitorial persecution traditionally fell into the hands of minority groups: Jews, driven out by the Catholic Kings' edict of expulsion of March 1492, the *converso* "crypto-Jews" persecuted by the Inquisition, and later the *moriscos,* of Muslim descent and custom though not, officially, religion.

Of course there were also Christian doctors practicing in Spain, among them surely practitioners who had been trained in the European schools of medicine at Salerno, Montpellier, and elsewhere from the thirteenth century on (Makdisi 261–279). While the diplomas and licenses accorded to these doctors afforded some reassurance to the patients as to their professional training and experience, there were nevertheless grave dangers inherent in medicine in an era before modern anesthetics and antibiotics. How much more so when the practitioners were not specialists in health, but in deception, chicanery, dialectic, and charlatan confidence games!

Medieval health care, by all reports, was a highly lucrative and risky business: lucrative for the doctor, that is, and risky for the patient. To fall ill in the Middle Ages was to run a double risk, that of the illness itself and what was often more deadly, the medical treatment. The bad doctor, the quack, the charlatan doctor all present a frequent and inviting target to satirists of all stripes, from Petrarch's *Invective contra medicum* to Molière's *Médecin malgré lui* or Doktor Eisenbart. In the Iberian Peninsula, Doctor Matasanos ["killer of the healthy"] prescribes the same deadly medicine, and Quevedo, for example, has this to say: "the unfortunate are killed by wounds, but the sick are killed by doctors" ["a los desgraciados mátanlos las heridas, a los enfermos mátanlos los médicos"] (134).

Nor are the dangers of European medicine described only in satirical texts. In a text that has been often anthologized and retold as an Arab witness to the Crusades (Gabrieli 76–77; Maalouf 147–148), a twelfth-century Damascene chronicler, Usāma ibn Munqid, relates the tale of a Frankish (that is, European) knight who was both unfortunate and ill, a tale that provides a chilling picture of the poor state of Western medicine at the time. The knight had nothing more than an abscess in his leg, which an Arab doctor, a Christian named Ṯābit, had already treated by means of a lotion. But afterwards there appeared a Frankish doctor who said to the patient: "This man knows nothing of medicine. Do you wish to live with one leg, or to die with two?" The poor knight, of course, deferring to the authority of the doctor, answered that he preferred to live, with both legs or one. Unfortunately, upon amputating the leg (again, with neither anesthetic nor antibiotics), the axe stroke was not cleanly delivered and had to be repeated, from which the poor patient expired on the spot, losing, after all that, his leg as well as his life. As the proverb says: "Kill the dog to stop the rabies" ["Muerto el perro, se acabó la rabia"].

This story is followed by another in which a woman suffers the same fate at the same doctor's hands for a case of mental derangement, which the Arab doctor treats by recommending dietary modifications, and the Frankish doctor attempts to relieve by incising the scalp and rubbing the wound with salt, a treatment that proved to be as deadly as it must have been painful. Both of Usāma's medical narratives serve to demonstrate the Arabs' cultural and intellectual superiority over the Franks at a time when both sides were intermittently at war with one another. It is still important to underline the fact that these two doctors differ not in religion, as both are Christians, but only in their language, culture, and especially their professional training and knowledge. One of them, the Arab, no doubt was practiced and familiar with Greek and Arabic treatises of medicine, while the other one, "barbarian" that he was, knew only how to operate, and even that he did badly.

But to return for a moment to the Frankish doctor's original question to his patient: "Do you wish to live with one leg, or to die with two?" The question reveals the doctor's unfortunate ignorance in medical matters, but points to a certain expertise in another discipline, that of dialectic, the art of logical persuasion, and in the rhetorical techniques of learned disputation of the *sic et non* type that were developed to perfection in the French schools by such masters as Peter Abelard, but not in medical centers such as Salerno and Montpellier (Nepaulsingh; Makdisi 261–262). Conversely, Ṭābit, the Arab doctor, seems to care less for theoretical medicine than for the empirical result, based on practical training and his own experience. These two attitudes toward medicine will again enter into competition in thirteenth-century Spain, in the satirical critiques of deadly doctors and their useless knowledge, a critique that will be summed up centuries later in the very different context of *gaucho* literature when Martín Fierro says:

> Doctors mean nothing here,
> only experience counts;
> here the know-it-alls
> would discover their innocence,
> because this has a different key,
> and the *gaucho* has his own science.

> [Aquí no valen dotores:
> sólo vale la esperiencia;
> aquí verían su inocencia

esos que todo lo saben,

porque esto tiene otra llave

y el gaucho tiene su cencia] (Hernández, lines 1457–1462)

In the CEM's poetics of equivocation and concealment, the social and cultural parameters that inform their jokes are nowhere so clear as they are in Usāma's chronicle of the Crusade and in the *gaucho*'s frontier territory. To show how the process of joking concealment functions, and what it reveals under analysis, it will first be necessary to outline some aspects of medieval medical practice, and then to examine how the CEM employ literary tropes to satirize the practitioners of medicine, before arriving at the hidden motive or kernel of their attacks.

Medical practitioners came from various social strata. At the level of most prestige were the university-trained masters and doctors: the master physician, *medicus physicus,* whose medical knowledge, like the astrologer's knowledge of the stars, composed part of a general study of natural philosophy (French 33–37; Siraisi 374–377). The master surgeon, *medicus chirugicus,* was trained in the more practical applications of surgery, a distinction that medical specialization makes to this day. Occupying a lower social sphere, the barber had even less formal training, and performed many functions besides that of cutting hair, including blood-letting, and cupping [*ventosas*] (another practice that continues today in many areas). He was also a dentist, inasmuch as extracting teeth was one of his trades. There were besides many other types of unofficial medical practice, from *curanderismo* and quackery to home remedies and midwifery, the domain especially of knowledgeable old women. Here the touchstone can be none other than Fernando de Rojas's Celestina, who according to Sempronio practiced six trades: "embroiderer, perfumer, expert in cosmetics and making virgins, procuress, and a little bit sorceress" ["labrandera, perfumera, maestra de fazer afeytes é de fazer virgos, alcahueta é un poquito hechizera"], apart from being or at least considering herself a pediatrician ["física de niños"] (60–61). It must be borne in mind that midwife and *celestina* were not the only "health care" professions available to women, as there were also trained women doctors — called *magistrae, fisicae, medicae, chirugicae* — who in some historians' count composed up to ten percent of all medical practitioners (Shatzmiller 108–112), or at least a "significant portion" thereof (Green 352).

In the Arcipreste de Hita's *Libro de buen amor*, it is Doña Garoza who tells a fable that puts on display the entire spectrum of medieval health care professionals. Another version of the same fable is included in the *Conde Lucanor* (*exemplo* 29), but the "logical tendency" of Don Juan Manuel's version does not offer the same richness of detail about fourteenth-century urban life as Juan Ruiz's (Menéndez Pidal, *Poesía árabe* 155). The fable runs as follows: a fox is trapped within the town walls by the town's inhabitants and, as there is no escape, the fox resolves to play dead as a last resort, come what may:

A shoemaker came by very early. "That's a fine-looking tail," he said, "and worth good money. Out of that, I can make a shoe horn to ease the shoes on." He cut it, but she, still as a lamb, did not make a move.

Then came the barber, returning from a blood-letting. "That tusk of hers would be fine for someone with tooth-ache or a sore jaw." He pulled her tooth, but she lay quiet, without a whimper.

An old woman came; the fox had eaten one of her hens. The old woman said, "her eye would make a good charm for girls who are bewitched or who are going through their pains." She removed the fox's eye, but that wretch did not dare move a muscle.

Then the physician came down the street. He said, "This fox's ear would be very good in cases of poisoning or for ear-ache." He cut them off, but she lay qui[e]ter than a sheep. Then the master said, "The heart of the fox is very useful for people who have palpitations."

But the fox cried, "Hell, take the devil's pulse!" and

jumping up, she ran off down the moat. (English trans. Migani and Di Cesare 272–273)

[Passava de mañana por í un çapatero: '¡O!,' diz, '¡qué buena cola! Más vale que un dinero: faré trainel della para calçar ligero.' Cortóla e estudo más queda que un cordero.

El alfajem passava, que venié de sangrar; diz: 'El colmillo désta puede aprovechar para quien dolor tiene en muela o en quexar.' Sacóle el diente e estudo queda, sin se quexar.

Una vieja passava que'l comió su gallina; diz: 'el ojo de aquésta es para melezina a moças aojadas o que an la madrina.' Sacójelo e sossegada estudo la mesquina.

El físico passava por aquesta calleja, diz: '¡qué buenas orejas son las de la golpeja para quien tien venino o dolor en la oreja!' Cortólas e estudo queda más que un oveja.

Dixo este maestro: 'el coraçón del raposo es mucho al tremor del coraçón provechoso.' Ella diz: '¡al diablo catedes vos el polso!' Levantóse corriendo e fuxo por el cosso.] (Juan Ruiz 1415–1419)

The first passerby is a cobbler, who cuts off the fox's tail for his shoes. Later, there arrives an *alfajeme,* the Hispano-Arabic name given to the barber, from the Arabic *al-ḥajjām* 'leech'. As the text indicates, this barber had just let a patient's blood ("venié de sangrar"). Upon encountering the fox, he extracts a tooth, saying that it relieves the pain of toothache. Tooth extraction and pain-killing, of course, are another of the offices of this barber, leech, dentist, cupper, *alfajeme, al-ḥajjām.* After the leech, an old woman passes by, plucking out the fox's eye and saying that it is useful for young women who have been bewitched by the evil eye as well as against menstrual cramps ("moças aojadas o que an la madrina"). The fact that she uses the same remedy for both types of illness affords yet another example of the bawd's peculiar combination of magic and medicine. After a while, a physician shows up, elsewhere referred to as a master and a surgeon ("físico," "maestro," surgiano"). He cuts off the fox's ear, as a remedy for otic diseases. But when the doctor is about to cut out the fox's heart, which according to him is beneficial for cardiac arrhythmias, the animal finally loses patience with so much bodily abuse, and runs away. "Go take the devil's pulse!" she says, referring to one of the fundamental means of medieval diagnosis of the Galenic tradition: taking the pulse, and observing the color of the urine. As the anonymous thirteenth-century treatise, *Summa pulsuum,* relates: "Of all the indications of the internal disposition of the body, two are most reliable, the pulse and the urine" (745). Or, as the proverb of Correas says more crudely, "clear urine and firm stools, signs of a steady pulse" ["Mear claro y cagar duro, señal de estar bueno el pulso"].

In every case (at least in the fable), it is interesting to remark, treatments are proposed in which the remedy applied is the same organ as the affected area (not counting the cobbler, naturally, who only considers the utilitarian value of the fox's tail). Fox teeth are good against toothache, fox eye against the evil eye, fox ear against diseases of the ear, fox heart for cardiac abnormality. Luis Granjel considers this passage of the *Libro de buen amor* representative of popular medical conceptions of the time (152–153). The theory of the microcosm's bodily humors and its equivocal correspondence "by analogy" with external nature remains, at least in the popular imagination, the basis of the medical practice of university-trained physicians and surgeons as well as of barbers, leeches, and midwives (Foucault, *The Order of Things* 32–33).

Indeed, there seems to be little difference in the kinds of treatment that each class of medical practitioner provides; and probably little difference, too, in the efficacy of each cure. The probability of a patient getting better is thought to have been the same under any of the health-care regimes:

> Moreover, it is, of course, unlikely that in the period under consideration the possessors of medical degrees could ever have been consistently more successful than any of their various competitors in effecting cures (although it is equally

unlikely that the contrary was the case). It seems probable, too, that a good many remedies were more or less common to several categories of practitioner. (Siraisi 363)

The haphazard quality and outcomes of medical interventions is again summed up in the *Libro de buen amor* in reference to the Arcipreste's own case of love-sickness: "The [medical] arts often help, other times they fail, / many survive by these arts, but many perish" ["las artes muchas vegadas ayudan, otras fallecen, / por las artes biven muchos e por las artes perecen"] (s. 591). Where there was a very noticeable difference, however, was in the fee charged by each of these practitioners, and hence in the social prestige that attached to their patients. "Por las artes biven muchos": this applies not only to the patients lucky enough to survive, but also to the doctors' livelihood earned from the practice of their arts. It is a bit disconcerting to imagine that these medics were competing more in the arena of the *qué dirán* of public opinion than in healing itself.

Given this predominantly social function of medicine, it comes as no surprise that each of these professional categories comes up as a target in the satires of the CEM. The poets of *escarnho* criticize old women, midwives, and bawds, as well as barbers, but their most biting satires are reserved for the university-trained doctors and masters of medicine.

(Against midwives:) An important episode in the burlesque songbook is the so-called "scandal of maids and weavers" [*amas e tecedeiras*], which treats, with the sexual insinuation and abased comicality characteristic of the CEM, the question of whether it is possible to love according to the precepts of courtly love a woman who is not of the nobility. A central tenet of the ideology of *fin'amors* is, of course, that the object of love-service must be of higher social station than the lover; and the satires partly depend on the obvious equivocation of the substantive *ama* 'maid' and the verb *ama* 'he loves'. Often overlooked, however, is another equivocal sense of *ama*, used to refer to the office of brothel-keeper, which furnishes a parallel interpretation of this scandal as one of brothel-keepers and prostitutes. One *cantiga* in ironic praise of an *ama* reveals the manifest zones of rusticity and domesticity in which her extra-official medical practices are located. The *ama,* according to CEM 130, knows how to cook weave, sew, and clean; her husband is an expert in castrating pigs and cocks — an indirect warning to the poet who is sleeping with his wife. She, in addition to her "domestic" skills, also knows how to cast the evil (but also erotic) eye ("escanta ben per olho") and is also and adept in other arts that in one way or another combine the medicine of home remedies with Celestina-like herbal, sexual and magical practices.

The CSM depict a similar instance of such arts, here love-magic, practiced by women (Zaid). In CSM 104, a Galician concubine [*barragana*] sacrilegiously uses a Eucharistic host as a love-charm [*amadoira*] to make her lover marry her. In keeping with the dialectic of praise and blame proper to the CSM, the sorceress is castigated by the Virgin for this sacrilege, where the CEM would have instead offered mocking praise.

(Against leeches:) One *cantiga* is directed against a certain "sangrador de Leirea," who stands accused of groping and fondling his patients and customers; as the refrain states, "fucked is the one who lets a leech leech him down there!" ["al fodido irá sangrar / sangrador en tal logar!"] (CEM 202). The poem is ironic, employing such clever parasynthetic condensations as *sofaldrar* 'to raise the skirt' (Brea), but these apparently humorous gestures only serve to mask an underlying tension that is much more serious: the patient's fear of doctors' power over the body, in their authoritative access to his personal intimacy. This is rendered clearly in the great legal code originated by Alfonso X, the *Siete partidas.* One title explains how the king's physicians must be, emphasizing that one of the most important characteristics is that they be extremely loyal, because, as the text states, "if they are not loyal, they will commit greater treason than other men, for the reason that they commit it in secret [. . .] as men who perfidiously kill others who trust in them" ["si leales no fueren farian mayores trayçiones que otros onbres porque las farian encubiertamente . . .] (2.9.10). In fact, there have been documented historical cases of medieval doctors who abused their patients, a crime that was considered terrible by both ecclesiastical and secular authorities (Shatzmiller

78–93), especially when the doctor was of a religion different from that of the patient, a situation generally prohibited by law. There was at times a particular fear and mistrust of Jewish doctors. Alfonso de Espina, for example, repeats a pernicious and patently false accusation against Don Meir Alguadex, that he desecrated the Eucharist and tried to poison the king, Enrique III, whose royal physician he was (Baer vol. 2, 288, 488n29). It will become apparent below that the question of minority doctors in Christian Spain is potentially the most conflicted site of medical sociology, and that this fear of the medical other offers a key to the cultural interpretation of the CEM's poetics of equivocation.

CEM 282 provides an example of how this equivocal poetics of combination operates. Here a doctor named Master Acenço has killed a knight in the city of Roda (La Roda) using, we are given to understand, his tenuous knowledge of medicine. But the *cantiga* manages to combine the topical satire of the deadly doctor with another, political thrust: the revolt against Alfonso X, led by the king's own son don Sancho. Since Roda was held by followers of Sancho, the poet Martín Moxa (a cleric from Santiago loyal to the royal party) speaks of the medical homicide as if it were no professional mistake, but rather an intentional result of military combat. The *cantiga*'s joke resides in the contrast between these combined hybrid elements: the doctor as knight, medicine as a weapon, incompetence as heroic valor.

Another satirical topic arises here: the avaricious doctor. Maestre Acenço's dilemma is that by killing the knight in Roda, he naturally is unable to charge him for his services. Another Alfonsine legal code, the *Fuero Real*, stipulates that physicians who directly or indirectly cause a patient's death cannot thereafter demand payment from the victim's family (Pimental 152). Martín Moxa, therefore, is ironically offering the incompetent doctor another possible source of revenue, the reward for military service.

The figure who best played the part of the deadly doctor was a certain Master Nicholas, who is called in one *cantiga* a bad doctor, "medico mao" (CEM 334) (Torres Fontes; Alvar, "Maestre Nicolás"; Michaëlis, *Cancioneiro da Ajuda* vol. 2, 534–538). A bad doctor, perhaps, but positively a genius in finding ways to separate a patient from his money. He uses herbs to render the living dead and the sane crazy; for the blind he prescribes a cane with which to guide themselves. He is able to make the dumb no longer speak, and the lame not rise. His specialty is to bring about these types of pseudo-miraculous cures that are neither miracles nor cures, but rather just the opposite. His art consists of always retaining his part of the profit. One of his techniques is thaumaturgy, curing by touch, but unlike the Niño Fidencio or medieval French kings, who had this power (Marc Bloch), his hand serves not to cure but to rob the credulous patient.

The laws of the *Siete partidas* paint a portrait of just this sort of physician:

> Some men profess to be more learned in medicine and surgery than they are, and it happens at times, for the reason that they are not so well informed as they say they are, sick or wounded persons die through their fault.

> [Métense algunos omes por mas sabidores que non son en física e en cirugia: e acaesce á las vegadas que porque non son tan sabidores como facen muestra, mueren algunos homes enfermos ó llagados por culpa dellos.] (7.8.6)

Just like the Frankish doctor in Usāma's tale who asks his patient, "Do you prefer to live with one leg, or to die with two?," the real talent of the charlatan doctor Master Nicholas is not medicine but dialectic. He knows how to conceal himself as much by his way of speaking as by his manner of dress. Everything for this simulacrum of a doctor is image and appearance. In CEM 42, he wears a cap of an Eastern sage, "capelo d'Ultramar," and carries Latin books from Montpellier that he cannot read. In this way he pretends to possess a two-fold medical training: on one hand, in the private tutorials of the Arab world; and on the other, in the medical school of Montpellier, one of the most renowned centers of medical teaching at the time, at one point even surpassing the reputation for medicine of Salerno (Siraisi 364–367). Master Nicholas's double formation in medicine corresponds to the organization of the new universities in thirteenth-century Spain, where Alfonso X founded in Seville two parallel universities, one for studies in Latin and the other for Arabic. To fill the positions in the medical school of the Arabic university, he had to resort to inviting foreign professors from the Arab world, who no doubt wore "capelos d'Ultramar" just like that of Master Nicholas, but whose formidable medical knowledge surely outstripped his own meager learning (Márquez Villanueva, *El concepto* 158).

In medieval Spain, then, there co-existed both traditions of medical lore. Here, however, in contrast to the story told by Usāma of the Frankish knight and his two doctors — both Christians — religious difference plays a central part, along with culture and professional curriculum. In Christian Spain, the practice of medicine was closely tied to the situation of religious minorities with respect to the dominant Christian culture, in those years of what may be called the late Reconquest "cultural synthesis" of the thirteenth century, under the patronage and guidance, as mentioned above, of kings such as Alfonso X and Denis of Portugal.

"Are there no doctors in Spain?" inquires naively Thornton Wilder's Marquesa de Montemayor. Medieval Spanish physicians were in large part Jewish. Jewish scholars in al-Andalus were the only ones who possessed both access to technical literature in Arabic as well as a certain degree of professional tolerance on the part of the newly arrived Christian conquerors. This period has been characterized as one of the "medicalization" of medieval society throughout Europe, due in large part to the notable difference in efficacy between Arab and European medical knowledge and by the consequent rise in expectations of medical services in light of formal medical learning (Shatzmiller 1–13; McVaugh, 190–191, 218–235) that was principally found in Arabic-language sources (García-Ballester, "A Marginal Learned Medical World"; Shatzmiller 38–42). A great many of the royal physicians of Castilian and Portuguese courts were Jews, who served also as intimates and counsellors to the kings (Baer, vol. 1, 121). One of them wrote a treatise of medicine entitled the *Book of Medicine of the Kings of Castile* [*Kitāb al-ṭibb al-qastālī al-malukī*] (García-Ballester, "A Marginal Learned Medical World" 376–390). The anonymous author, who identifies himself as a Jew, emphasizes the primacy of personal experience in treatment, along with the careful study of medical texts in Arabic. He reveals a very low opinion of Christian doctors, and says of doctors who do not know Arabic that it is better not to listen to them (377, 384–385).

But the aim here and in the CEM is not to speak of the deserved fame of such Hispano-Jewish and *converso* doctors and scholars as Ḥasdai ibn Shaprut, Petrus Alfonsi (author of the *Disciplina clericalis* [Hermes]), Maimonides, Todros ben Abulafia, and others (Granjel 99–107). Rather, it is to make sense of the very different Master Nicholas, charlatan doctor, and the satires directed against him and his ilk. It would be simple to dismiss the satires against this Christian doctor as mere jokes about the topical stereotype of bad doctors. There were besides many doctors with the same hardly uncommon name, from the "magister Nicolaus physicus" of Salerno onwards (Jacquart and Thomasset 32–35). Even in Don Quijote's unnamed town, the barber is named Maese Nicolás. (It is he who helps the priest in the inquisitorial burning of Don Quijote's library.) It would be easy to dismiss them, were it not for a disconcerting piece of historical evidence. Master Nicholas appears to have been a royal physician of high standing in the courts of Alfonso X, his rebellious son Sancho IV, Fernando IV, and even James II of Aragon (Torres Fontes). In the *Crónica de Alfonso Décimo* there is a dramatic moment when Alfonso (sick and practically on his deathbed) receives a premature notice of his rebellious son Sancho's death, news that later turns out to be false. The chronicle continues:

> And when his household saw that he had in this way distanced himself, they understood that he was showing his

great grief for the death of his son. Then one of his intimates, whom they called Master Nicholas, made bold to enter into the chamber where he was and say these words to
him: "Sir, why do you show such great grief for the Infante
don Sancho your son, whom you had disinherited? For if
the Infante don Juan and these other nobles who are here
with you should discover this, you will lose them all and
they will take some action against you." And the King, to
show that he was not weeping or grieving for don Sancho
and to hide his grief from them, responded, "Master Nicholas,
I am not weeping for the Infante don Sancho; rather I am
weeping for my own poor self, since now that he is dead I
shall never recover my kingdoms. . . ."

[É cuando los de su casa vieron que así estava apartado, en-
tendieron que mostraba grand pesar por la muerte de su fijo,
é atrevióse uno de los sus privados, que decian maestre
Nicolás, é entró á la cámara á él, é díjole estas palabras. "Señor,
¿por qué mostrades tan grand pesar por el infante don Sancho, vuestro fijo, que vos tenia desheredado? Ca si vos lo saben
el infante don Juan é estos otros ricos omes que son aquí con-
vusco, perderlos hedes todos, é tomarán alguna carrera contra
vos." É él por mostrar que non lloraba nin avia pesar por el infante don Sancho, é encobrir que le non entendiesen que
mostraba pesar por él, dijo estas palabras: "Maestre Nicolás:
non lloro yo por el infante don Sancho, mas lloro por mí,
mezquino viejo, que pues él muerto es, nunca yo cobraré los
mis reinos. . . ."] (*Crónica de Alfonso X* 65)

How has this charlatan, deadly doctor Master Nicholas reached such
a degree of confidence and intimacy with Alfonso in this tragic moment
of his reign? If medicine was a competitive profession, as would be ex-

pected given its high demand and potentially high rewards, how could Nicholas compete successfully with other doctors (especially Jewish doctors) whose medical competence was surely much greater than his own? How is it that he is the only one bold enough to address the king in these trying circumstances?

One *cantiga* offers a partial clue. More patients now go to Master Nicholas, the poet explains, than to Master Andreu, now that the latter has died: "mais van a el que a meestr' Andreu / des antano que o outro morreu" (CEM 42). Holding a monopoly seems to be the only advantage enjoyed by Master Nicholas. This charlatan Master's skills seem to be less in the field of medicine than in the fields of language: talking to the king in his time of greatest need, being taken into confidence, practicing the arts of counsel, dialectic, chicanery. This emphasis on language rather than the physical body leads into the hidden motive or kernel that the equivocal poetics of the CEM express "encubertamente." In the royal courts of late Reconquest Spain, despite the overwhelming presence of Jewish physicians, there was a particular niche for Christian doctors, even when their knowledge of medicine was far inferior to that of their Arabic-speaking Jewish colleagues.

The title of the *Siete partidas* on Jews prohibits any intimate association between members of different faiths. According to these laws and others (Carpenter; Granjel 99–100), which in practice must surely have been frequently contravened, Jews and Christians could not be married, not have sexual relations, not live under the same roof, not bathe together, not even eat or drink together. A slight exception is made for Jewish doctors, who, though they may not treat Christian patients directly, are permitted to do so by giving instructions through a Christian intermediary, who would seem in reality then to be little more than a medical assistant:

> We also order [. . .] that no Christian shall take any medi-
> cine or cathartic made by a Jew; but he can take it by the ad-

vice of some intelligent person, only when it is made by a Christian, who knows and is familiar with its ingredients.

[Otrosi defendemos que ningunt cristiano reciba melecinamiento ni purga que sea fecha por mano de judio; pero bien la puede recebir por consejo de algunt judio sabidor, solamente que sea fecha por mano de cristiano que conosca et entienda las cosas que son en ella.] (7.24.8)

While it was certainly possible, as these laws show, to imagine in theory a fully segregated society, even there the everyday realities of intercultural medical practice require the presence, at one remove, of Jewish apothecaries, doctors, and scholars.

The law obviously does not represent the actual state of society, but rather an idealizing desire of how it ought to or ought not to be. The poetry of *escarnho* and *mal dizer* presents the transgressive counterpart of the same phenomenon. If the law's prescriptions favor Christian doctors in supervisory capacities, the poetry of *escarnho*, in contrast, brings them down in its satires. If the law imposes a language of stable signification, even to the point of prohibiting the very *cantigas d'escarnho* themselves "por rimas e por escripto," then the equivocal language of *escarnho*, to the contrary, lets itself wander through the garden of forking paths.

Still far away is the bloody medicine of Calderon's *Médico de su honra*, far too the inquisitorial ideologies of honor, race, and purity of blood. But even in this late Reconquest thirteenth-century "cultural synthesis," there begin to appear, in law and in the transgressive and equivocal satires about deadly doctors, some of the social preoccupations surrounding religion, difference, and identity. These cultural anxieties are themselves born and defined in a complex and ambiguous negotiation of these two opposing desires and strategies of self-representation.

7

CONCLUSION

PROLOGUES TO A POETICS OF LAUGHTER

We overcome solitude by singing about it and we overcome
individual weakness by making fun of it. Before nature we
are lyrical; before other men, humorists.

[Vencemos la soledad cantándola y vencemos la debilidad
individual burlándonos de ella. Ante la naturaleza somos
líricos; ante los demás hombres, humoristas.]
— Ramón Piñeiro (ctd. in De la Vega 41)

In the preceding chapters, I have argued that the particular, individually
targeted critiques of the CEM respond to broader underlying zones of social tension in court society, whether cultural, intercultural, spiritual, or
hermeneutic. They do so, however, through the indirect poetics of *escarnho*, which prefers to speak its critiques through concealed words (*per
palavras cubertas*). Even when the *mal dizer* is more direct and plain-spoken
(*chaãmente*), it is circumscribed by a ludic space of permissible behaviors

that renders them rituals of courtly interchange; like the dialogued *tenço* 'debate poem' (< Latin *contentio*), these airings of poetic grievances, however tendentious, are still only verbal jokes, told within a restricted environment and moment that is appropriate to joking. As Freud remarks:

> [Jokes] restrict themselves, however, to a choice of occasions in which this play or this nonsense can at the same time appear allowable (in jests) or sensible (in jokes), thanks to the ambiguity of words and the multiplicity of conceptual structures. Nothing distinguishes jokes more clearly from all other psychical structures than this double-sidedness and this duplicity in speech. (*Jokes* 213–14)

Alfonso X's *Siete partidas* define with some precision when and in what manner such occasions for sensible play are permissible. The joke must be told so that all participants, the teller, the audience and also the butt of the joke, laugh and take pleasure in its telling (Filios 30, Liu 45–46). The legal text continues:

> Moreover, the one who tells [the joke] must know how to laugh in the appropriate place, for otherwise it would not be a game. For this reason the ancient proverb says there is no game when someone does not laugh.

> [Et otrosi el que lo dixiere que lo sepa bien reir en el logar do conviniere, ca de otra guisa non serie juego, et por eso dice el vierbo antiguo que non es juego onde home non rie.] (2.9.30)

The law suggests that even joking should be subject to legislation in time, place and manner ("in the appropriate place" ["en el logar do conviniere"]), and that these rules of the game, moreover, are necessary in order to maintain the very playfulness of the game itself. One of Alfonso's own *cantigas* cites a similar version of the same proverb, when a cowardly no-bleman says "it is no game if it makes someone cry!" ["non é jog' o de que omen chora!"] (CEM 16)

This opposition between laughter and tears, along with the corre-sponding opposition between humor and lyric (De la Vega 41, 72–76), is crucial to locating the "appropriate place" of joking, which is negotiated between the Scylla of frivolity and the Charbydis of seriousness. Henri Bergson, in his classic study on laughter, *Le rire: essai sur la signification du comique* (first published in 1899) had already noted the peculiar *insensi-bilité* 'insensitivity' or 'indifference' of laughter, which is produced only in the absence of feeling. He writes: "Indifference is its natural environment. Laughter has no greater foe than emotion" ["L'indifférence est son milieu naturel. Le rire n'a pas de plus grand ennemi que l'émotion"] (3). Laugh-ter, and the "comic spirit" ["esprit comique"] that generates it, is for Berg-son above all an intellectual and social substitute for feeling.

Freud, only a few years later, in the final part of his 1905 work on *Jokes and their Relation to the Unconscious,* gives a rather different twist to Berg-son's notion of "esprit comique," though not as some form of innate wit, "comic spirit," or, again quoting Bergson, "an extremely subtle essence that evaporates when exposed to the light" (105). Freud instead chooses to analyze the more approachable "mot d'esprit," the verbal wit that oper-ates in language as the unconscious does in dreams. However, Freud also recognizes humor and laughter as an avoidance of feeling, a screen or mask that takes the place of unpleasant emotions. As he puts it, "the plea-sure of humour . . . comes about . . . at the cost of a release of affect that does not occur: it arises from an economy in expenditure of affect" (*Jokes* 284) or "feeling" (*Jokes* 293). He repeats this formulation in another short piece on humor in 1927: "the yield of humorous pleasure arises from an economy in expenditure upon feeling" ("Humour" 161). Freud cites in this regard the example of "gallows humor," in which laughter covers over the seriousness of emotion in general, which in this case takes the specific form of pity: for instance, when a prisoner who is being led to the gallows to be hanged asks for a scarf so as not to catch cold on the way (*Jokes* 285). Now if we laugh at the absurdity of the proposition, it is because rather than imitate the expected emotional reaction, pity, we have been led to laugh at how that expectation has been deflected by the prisoner's or the joke-teller's humorous misdirection of it. Humor, for Freud in his 1927 article, can thus become a kind of liberating and rebellious triumph of the pleasure principle (163) that puts the pleasure of laughter in the place where feeling was expected.

The antagonism between humor and feeling, laughter and tears, also connects with the poetics of laughter in the medieval *cancioneros*. The poetry of laughter is frequently presented as a counterpoint to the lyric of suffering, for example to the painful languishing desire of the *coita d'amor* that is so prevalent in Galician-Portuguese and courtly love lyric generally. It is in this sense, too, that the *cantigas d'escarnho e de mal dizer*, as songs of laughter, stand in opposition to the gendered lyric genres of the masculine *cantiga d'amor* and the feminine *cantiga d'amigo*. The later Portuguese *Cancioneiro Geral de Garcia de Resende* (1516) has only two thematic partitions: the love lyric is entitled "of suffering and sighing" ["de cuidar e sospirar"], while the other is marked as "things for enjoyment" ["cousas de folguar"], consisting largely of jokes, invectives and some obscenities.

Lyric, as is well known, can itself constitute a substitute for feeling that derives poetic pleasure from the experience of suffering. Gracián writes that "there is a beautiful harmony between singing and crying" ["Hay una dulcísima armonia entre el cantar y llorar"] (22). The opening verses of *Martín Fierro* are but one of many examples of this association:

> Now shall I sing
> to the rhythm of the *vihuela*,
> for, like the solitary bird,
> the man who lets loose
> his extraordinary suffering
> consoles himself in song.

[Aquí me pongo a cantar
al compás de la vigüela,
que el hombre que lo desvela
una pena estrordinaria,
como la ave solitaria
con el cantar se consuela.] (Hernández ll. 1–6)

Similarly, in an actual song tradition, the flamenco singer Camarón de la Isla, sings:

I am like the sad bird
who sings his sorrows
because he knows not how to cry.

[Soy como el pájaro triste
que canta sus penas
porque no sabe llorar.]

"Cantar las penas," singing one's sorrows, singing the blues, even evoking the happy state of nature in the song of birds: these are poetic antidotes to emotional pain. In the same way, but more indirectly, to laugh, or even to shed tears of laughter, is a way of crying without having to shed "real" tears of grief. "Humor is the tip of tragedy," the Moroccan political humorist Ahmed Sannousi (Bziz) has said. Freud calls this type "broken" humor, which he describes as "the humour that smiles through tears" (*Jokes* 289).

Perhaps the greatest advocate and provoker of laughter, François Rabelais, advises:

It is better to write about laughter than about tears
For laughter is the mark of man.

Mieux est de ris que de larmes escripre
Pour ce que le rire est le propre de l'homme. (Ménager 12)

Rabelais makes reference here to the medieval neo-Aristotelians, for whom man was distinguished as the *animal risibile,* the animal capable of laughter (Liu 44). Aristotle himself had written, in the *Parts of Animals,* that man is "the only animal that laughs. . . . [N]o animal but man ever laughs" (673a6–27), though the laughter he describes seems to be induced more by physiological means than by social or poetic ones. In any case, as Umberto Eco's novel *The Name of the Rose* reminds us, lacking Aristotle's book on comedy, it is uncertain whether there could be a medieval science of laughter.

Even in the absence of the Philosopher's authority, however, some fragmentary clues as to vernacular poetic practices involving laughter, wit, joking, and the substitution of feeling are furnished by a series of prologues that introduce various collections of poetry which, like the *cantigas d'escarnho e de mal dizer,* record, however faintly, the echoing peals of laughter in medieval Iberia.

These highly varied medieval Iberian poetic compilations, ranging from the twelfth to the early sixteenth century, include texts in Castilian, Galician-Portuguese, and even Hispano-Arabic, reveal in their witty jokes — and more particularly in the prologues that introduce them — certain shared preoccupations concerning the social and literary status of such joke poetry. These prefatory texts include, first, Ibn Quzmān's prologue to his colloquial Hispano-Arabic *dīwān* in twelfth-century Muslim Córdoba. Second, the fourteenth-century *arte de trovar* or *ars poetica* that introduces the corpus of non-devotional poetry in Galician-Portuguese, as discussed in this book. Third, the Marqués de Santillana's brief history of poetry through the mid-fifteenth century that is his famous *Proemio e carta,* though this text takes quite a different perspective from the rest. Fourth, the "Prologus Baenensis," Juan Alfonso de Baena's prologue to his Castilian *cancionero,* compiled around 1430. Fifth, Hernando del Castillo's prologue to his printed *Cancionero general* of 1511, and lastly Garcia de Resende's Portuguese *Cancioneiro Geral* of the same decade.

Many of these prologues seem to make paradoxical claims for, on one hand, the inherent aesthetic merit of the compiled joke works, but also for the linguistic and cultural specificity of the in-group that would have access to the joke poems' complex modes of signification. Laughter, like language, establishes communities that participate in it and define themselves in part through it. "Laughter goes by neighborhoods" ["la risa va por barrios"], or to cite Bergson: "our laughter is always the laughter of a group" ["notre rire est toujours le rire d'un groupe"] (5).

However, it is also possible to trace some curious connections in the language of laughter across communities. Evidence for one such transcultural journey is furnished in the etymology of the Spanish word *carcajada*, meaning "guffaw." The word derives from the Arabic verb *qahqaha*, a quadriliteral root that, much like "guffaw," imitates in language the throaty sounds of laughter by repeating the glottal *qaf* and the aspirated *ha*. This onomatopoeic duplication in language is characteristic of an entire class of quadriliteral verbal roots in Arabic: for example, the word meaning "to whisper" is *waswasa*. But how to account, then, for the Spanish borrowing of *carcajada* from Arabic? After all, as the sixteenth-century expatriate humanist Juan de Valdés informs us in his 1535 *Diálogo de la lengua*, Arabisms in Castilian indicate novel things introduced to Spain by the Arabs: "you will find that only for those things that we have taken from the Moors have we no other words by which to name them except the Arabic ones that [the Moors] introduced along with the things themselves" ["hallaréis que para solas aquellas cosas, que avemos tomado de los moros, no tenemos otros vocablos con que nombrarlas sino los arávigos que ellos mesmos con las mesmas cosas nos introduxeron"] (30). It is of course a philosophical question as to the precedence of being and being named, of words and things. Should we believe, with Juan de Valdés, that borrowing the word for *carcajada* indicates as well a borrowing of the practice?

There is a singular witness to the poetry of laughter in al-Andalus, namely the sole manuscript of the *diwān* of Ibn Quzmān of Córdoba, the master of *zajal* poetry in colloquial Hispano-Arabic. In his prologue, written in classical Arabic in rhymed prose (*saj*'), he contrasts the "plain language" of his introduction with the wittiness of the *azjāl* to follow: "We leave off plain language and coin wittiness and rare jests with an un-stumbling tongue" ["naqṭa'u l-kalāma l-manṯūr, wa-naṭba'u l-milḥa wa-n-nawādira bi-lisānin ġayri 'aṯūr"] (*Gramática*, Ar. 6). Federico Corriente nicely translates the terms *milḥ* and *nawādir* (sing. *nādir*) into Spanish as "sales y donaires" (Ibn Quzmān, *Cancionero* 40). The former word, trans-lated here as "wittiness," means literally saltiness, but with the secondary meaning of witty speech; a usage that exists in Spanish, as in Corriente's rendering, in the loan translation of *malīḥ* as "salado," which preserves both senses of "salty" and "witty." Ibn Quzmān further explains in his prologue the techniques he has used to create the *zajal*'s complex poetry of wit:

> I made [the *zajal*] difficult for uncivilized natures to grasp. . . . I made it close and distant, ordinary and strange, difficult and easy, concealed and obvious.

> [Wa-ṣa"abtu 'alà l-'aġlafi l-ṭab'a wuṣūla-h . . . wa-ja'altu-hu qarīban ba'īdan, wa-baladiyyan ġarīban, wa-ṣa'ban hayyi-nan, wa-ġāmiḍan bayyinan.] (*Gramática*, Ar. 1)

The word for "uncivilized," *aġlaf*, actually has the literal meaning "un-circumcised." What is here rendered "ordinary and strange" is in Arabic "baladiyyan ġarīban," where the Spanish *baladí*, in the sense of "banal," is readily recognizable. These two Arabic words could also be translated, not as "ordinary and strange," but also as "local and foreign" or even "native and stranger."

What Ibn Quzmān seems to be describing in his prologue is a playful poetry of wit that segregates his audience, presumably composed of both native Andalusis (born in Muslim Spain) and the invading Almohad rulers from North Africa, by virtue of their linguistic and cultural competence or belonging. Or perhaps the word *aġlaf* should be taken literally to mean "the uncircumcised" and, in combination with Ibn Quzmān's Visigothic patronymic (Guzmán), to be directed against Mozarab Christian communities in al-Andalus. In either event, it is clear that polysemous language and the peculiar poetry of laughter here combine to identify competing groups for inclusion or exclusion according to interpretative ability. Through the kind of ambiguous misdirection that Ibn Quzmān describes in his prologue, his meanings are expressed only indirectly, articulated only in language that is equivocal, combinatory, substitutive, hybrid, in an artful concealment that is motivated, at least in part, by the interests of self-preservation.

If the laughter of jokes can positively constitute a community's way of talking about itself to itself, to name itself, to point to itself, even to criticize itself, it can also divide based on ethnicity, gender, religion, nationality, region, dress, sexuality, social class, food, age, circumcision, or any other sign of difference. To return for a moment to Bergson and Freud, it is on this point that they really part company in interpreting laughter. For Bergson the laughter caused by jokes maintains the group and acts above all as a normalizing social corrective (15); while for Freud the very pleasure of laughter lies in how it expresses and deflects the animosity and aggressiveness that underlie such categorically tendentious jokes (*Jokes* 121–23, 214).

Ibn Quzmān's description of his poetry of polysemous wittiness bears an uncanny resemblance (to borrow his own words, *baladiyyan ġarīban* 'familiar but strange') to that of the Galician-Portuguese *cantigas d'escarnho e de mal dizer* that have been discussed in the preceding chapters. The anonymous *arte de trovar* that prefaces the songs collected in the CBN manuscript associates them with the genre of laughter-producing songs known as *cantigas de risabelha*:

> But it is also said that there are others, [songs] of *risabelha,*
> which can be either of *escarnho* or of *mal dizer*. These are so

called because men often laugh at them, but there is no wisdom or other good in them.

[pero er dizẽ que outras ha hy de risabelha, estas ou seerã
d'escarnho ou de mal dizer, e chaman-lhes asy por que riiẽ
ende a vezes os homẽs, mays nõ som cousas ẽ que sabedoria
nẽ outro bẽ aja.] (D'Heur, "*L'art de trouver*" 107)

Risabelha appears to derive from the Latin neuter plural *risibilia*
'things capable of laughter' or, since that is an exclusively human capabil-
ity, 'things capable of eliciting laughter'. In this sense the *cantiga de risabelha* would represent a vernacular parallel to the medieval Latin genre
of the *ridiculum* (Liu 44). The songs would thus elicit laughter by means
of the two tendentious poetic strategies of the CEM, either through direct
insult and invective, or through an artful concealment of purpose in
equivocal significations.

The *arte de trovar,* however, dismisses these compositions as entirely
frivolous pieces devoid of *sabedoria* 'wisdom', 'knowledge', 'artfulness', and
of any other good quality except that of making men laugh. The disap-
proving tone here is reminiscent of a later and much better known prologue, the Marqués de Santillana's *Proemio e carta,* one brief reference of
which bears comparison to the *arte de trovar*'s low estimation of *risabelha*. In this context, Santillana makes the classical distinction between
the sublime, mediocre, and low styles of poetry. But his interpretation
takes a different approach: the sublime is reserved for the ancients and the
mediocre for the practitioners of the gay science of poetry in vulgar
tongues, which he defines famously as "a fabrication of useful things"
["fingimiento de cosas útyles"] expressed in regular meters and forms. And
what purpose, use or other good ("outro ben," as the *arte de trovar* puts it)
can there be in things made only for the purpose of eliciting pleasure in
laughter, rather than in useful instruction in pleasant form (*utile dulce*)?

Such low poetry, which Santillana dismisses as "vain and lascivious things" ["cosas vanas e lascivas"], belongs exclusively to the basest social and aesthetic class:

> The lowest are those who, without order, measure, or meter, compose ballads and songs in which people of the base and servile class take delight.

> [Infimos son aquellos que syn ningund orden, regla nin cuento fazen romances e cantares de que las gentes de baxa e servil condición se alegran.] (210)

The noble, *linajudo* Santillana still speaks the old language of aristocratic privilege and hereditary feudal hierarchy. But even in the contemporary courts of the Trastámara kings, which included Santillana's personal *bête noire,* the illegitimate but powerful *condestable* Don Alvaro de Luna, new and different accents were beginning to be heard, which could also be cause for laughter.

It is Juan Alfonso de Baena who compiles (around 1430) many of these sounds in his *Cancionero de Baena,* and who outlines in its prologue a lengthy justification for idle pleasures and games, including those of the sort afforded by the some of the *cancionero*'s poems of invective, mockery, and insults that are traded amidst laughter.

> If Your Grace [King Juan II] should read this book at the appropriate times, you will find entertainment and enjoyment in it, and will take from it many delights, pleasures and satisfactions. Moreover, with all the pleasant, amusing and singular things written and contained within, your great and royal person will have rest and repose from labors, troubles and afflictions; and moreover, you will cast away, forget, distance and throw off from yourself all the sadness, cares, thoughts and burdens of the spirit that the many and

arduous affairs of state often bring on, cause and put upon
princes.

[si la su merçed en este dicho libro leyere en sus tiempos devidos, con él se agradará e deleitará e folgará e tomará muchos comportes e plazeres e gasajados. E aun otrosí, con las
muy agradables e graçiosas e muy singulares cosas que en él
son escriptas e contenidas, la su muy redutable e real persona
averá reposo e descanso en los trabajos e afanes e enojos, e
otrosí desechará e olvidará e apartará e tirará de sí todas tris-
tezas e pesares e pensamientos e afliçiones del spíritu que
muchas devezes atraen e causan e acarrean a los prínçipes los
sus muchos e arduos negoçios reales.] (2)

Behind the accumulation of synonyms that amplify Baena's prose, his
message is readily apparent: the book offers a moment of recreation from
the gravity of kingship, the worries of which will be for a moment cast
away, forgotten, distanced, thrown off. What is interesting to remark in
the passage's rich synonymy is the balance that it establishes between the
light pleasures and the grave troubles to which those pleasures offer an alternative. On one side the words for enjoyment can be weighed: *deleitará,
folgará, comportes, plazeres, gasajados, agradables, graçiosas, singulares* (this
last reminiscent of Ibn Quzmān's *nawādir* 'rare jests'). On the other side,
in remarkable balance, the words for cares: *trabajos, afanes, enojos, tris-
tezas, pesares, pensamientos, afliçiones del spíritu, arduos negoçios.*

Baena's justification of the uses of pleasure recalls the general antago-
nisms metioned above between laughter and feeling, or humor and lyric.
Whereas Santillana separates these along the lines of social class, Baena
resolves the issue by appealing to a division of time into work time and
leisure time. "At the appropriate times" ["en sus tiempos devidos"], he
says to Juan II. This notion of compartmentalizing time, which Jacques Le
Goff has described as "the time of merchants" and "labor time" (29–52),

marks out a certain duration of leisure time for play, carefully delimited, in which laughter is considered not only acceptable but appropriate (*sus tiempos devidos*).

This marking off of the territory of laughter is even more pronounced in two later songbooks that bridge the medieval and early-modern periods. Garcia de Resende's Portuguese *Cancioneiro Geral* (1516), as mentioned above, is divided into two sections: serious pieces and ludic ones (*cousas de folguar*). More elaborately, the *Cancionero general* of Hernando del Castillo, first published in print in 1511, is roughly divided into nine large thematic categories. The overall plan, as Castillo writes in the prologue to the whole *cancionero,* was to organize the work into more or less the following sections: pieces of devotion and morality, love pieces arranged by author and title, songs, ballads, poetic competitions, amplified glosses, carols, questions, and, lastly, "works in jest that provoke laughter," ["obras de burlas provocantes a risa"] (Bellón and Jauralde Pou ix).

The justification provided in Del Castillo's prologue for this last section is in general quite similar to Baena's. Unlike Baena, however, who directly addresses his king and patron, Castillo addresses an unseen, imagined public of readers of printed works, whose weighty labors are not kingly but readerly. He proposes that the laughter-provoking section thus serve as a piquant refreshment to any monotony of reading the serious works that precede it:

> And to relieve any satiety that the many serious works above may have caused readers, I placed at the end the section of Jests that provoke laughter, with which the work concludes, so that by sections each may choose what most pleases his palate.

> [É por quitar el fastío á los lectores que por ventura las muchas obras graues arriba leydas les causaron, puse á la fin

las cosas de Burlas prouocantes á risa, con que concluye la obra, porque coja cada vno por órden lo que más agrada á su apetito.] (25)

In the new world of the printed book, it is the division into ordered chapters, rather than ordered hours of courtly activity, that determines the "appropriate" times and occasions for laugh-provoking entertainments.

The progressive compartmentalization of the poetry of laughter is in another sense completed when in 1519 the *Obras de burlas provocantes a risa* are published as a separatum volume, no longer attached to the "many serious works read above" ["las muchas obras graves arriba leidas"]. The leisure activities of laughing entertainments no longer accompany and balance the more serious endeavors, but now represent instead a potentially dangerous distraction from them.

The paradoxical closeness of laughter and tears, mentioned above regarding Freud's "broken" humor or "the laughter that smiles through tears," echoes here as well in the notes of desperation sounded in the prologues to these *cancioneros* of laughter. The very project of compiling songbooks, or for that matter jokebooks, bespeaks a fear of impending loss that the compiler seeks to compensate in writing. Baena, who is by profession a royal scribe, states this clearly in his prologue:

> For were it not through writings, what knowledge, what wit or memory of people could be remembered out of all that has gone before?
>
> [Ca si por las escripturas non fuesse, ¿quál sabiduría o quál engeño o memoria de omnes se podrié membrar de todas las cosas passadas?] (4)

"And for the same reason," writes Garcia de Resende in the prologue to his Portuguese songbook of 1516, "many things for enjoyment [*cousas de folguar*] and refinements have been lost without leaving notice of themselves. This is the reason behind the art of poetry [*trovar*]" ["e por esta mesma causa ... muytas cousas de folguar & gentylezas ssam perdydas ssem auer delas notyçia. No qual conto entra a arte de trovar"].

It is also the underlying reason in all these medieval Iberian prologues for compiling these lyrical songbooks and humorous jestbooks of laughter and tears. Though their jokes may no longer be funny or pleasurable to early-modern or late-modern readers, these *cancioneros* of *milḥ* and *nawādir*, "sales y donaires," wittiness and rare jests, of songs of *risabelha* or "laughables," of "many comforts, pleasures and entertainments" ["muchos comportes e plazeres e gasajados"], of "things of enjoyment" ["cousas de folguar"], and "laughter-provoking jokes" ["obras de burlas provocantes a risa"] all seek to preserve these jokes in writing and so to record the remembered moments of shared leisure and laughter in the past, in which according to Alfonsine law no one is to be injured. The retrospective work undertaken by these medieval compilers waxes far more nostalgic for a lost or disappearing community of laughter than the sharp, cutting, dividing verbal weapon that will be wielded in the early modern period under the names of *agudeza* and *ingenio* (Gracián, Chevalier, Casas Rigall, May).

BIBLIOGRAPHY

Ackerlind, Sheila R. *King Dinis of Portugal and the Alfonsine Heritage.* New York: Lang, 1990.

Aguiar, Manuel de. "Cantigas de Escárnio e Maldizer: uma Galeria de Caricaturas." *Portugaliae Historica.* 2 vols. Lisboa: Faculdade de Letras da Universidade de Lisboa, 1974. 2: 65–89.

Airas Nunez. *A poesía de Airas Nunez.* Ed. Giuseppe Tavini. Trans. Rosario Alvarez Blanco. Vigo: Galaxia, 1992.

Alfonso X, el Sabio. *Antología.* Ed. Antonio G. Solalinde. Buenos Aires: Espasa-Calpe, 1941.

———. *Cantigas de Santa María.* Ed. Walter Mettmann. 3 vols. Madrid: Castalia, 1986–1989.

———. *Las siete partidas del rey don Alfonso el Sabio.* 3 vols. Madrid: Real Academia de la Historia, 1807. English trans.: *Las Siete Partidas.* Trans. Samuel Parsons Scott. Chicago: Commerce Clearing House, 1931.

Alonso, Martín. *Diccionario medieval español: desde las Glosas Emilianenses y Silenses (s. X) hasta el siglo XV.* Salamanca: Universidad Pontificia de Salamanca, 1986.

Alonso Hernández, José Luis. "Juglaría, cazurrismo y carnaval." *La juglaresca: actas del I congreso internacional sobre la juglaresca.* Ed. Manuel Criado de Val. Madrid: EDI-6, 1986. 131–137.

Alvar, Carlos. "Maestre Nicolás y las cantigas de escarnio gallego-portuguesas." *Revista de Literatura* 43 (1981): 133–140.

————. "María Pérez, Balteira." *Archivo de Filología Aragonesa* 36–37 (1986): 11–40.

Alvar, Carlos and Vicente Beltrán, eds. *Antología de la poesía gallego-portuguesa.* Madrid: Alhambra, 1989.

Álvares, Cristina and Americo Lindeza Diogo. "La lyrique galégo-portugaise, l'influence provençale et le cas des pastourelles." *Contacts de langues, de civilisations et intertextualité.* Troisième Congrès Internationale d'Études Occitanes (Montpellier, 20–26 septembre 1990). Ed. Gérard Gouiran. Montpellier: Centre d'Études Occitanes, 1990. 738–751.

Alzieu, Pierre, Robert Jammes and Yvan Lissorgues. *Floresta de poesías eróticas del siglo de oro.* Toulouse: Université de Toulouse-Le Mirail, 1975.

Amigo, Fernando M. "El tema amoroso en la poesía de Pedr'Amigo de Sevilla." See Carreño, *Actas.* 115–123.

Anglade, Joseph, ed. *Las flors del gay saber.* Barcelona: Institut d'Estudis Catalans, 1926.

Aristotelis Latinus. *Categoriae vel Praedicamenta.* Ed. L. Minio-Paluello. Oxford: Clarendon, 1966.

Aristotle. *Categories.* Trans. E. M. Edghill. *The Basic Works of Aristotle.* Ed. Richard McKeon. New York: Random House, 1941. 3–37.

————. *On Rhetoric: A Theory of Civic Discourse.* Trans. George A. Kennedy. New York: Oxford University Press, 1991.

Asensio, Eugenio. *Poética y realidad en el cancionero peninsular de la Edad Media.* Biblioteca Románica Hispánica (II. Estudios y ensayos), 34. 2nd ed. Madrid: Gredos, 1970.

Ashworth, E. J. "A Thirteenth-Century Interpretation of Aristotle on Equivocation and Analogy." *Aristotle and His Medieval Interpreters.* Canadian Journal of Philosophy, supplementary vol. 17. Ed. Richard Bosley and Martin Tweedale. Calgary: University of Calgary Press, 1992. 85–101.

Averçó, Luis de. *Torcimany.* Ed. José María Casas Homs. 2 vols. Barcelona: Consejo Superior de Investigaciones Científicas, 1956. Vol. 1.

Averroes. *Middle Commentary on Aristotle's Categories.* Ed. Mahmoud M. Kassem. Cairo: General Egyptian, 1980. [English trans.: *Averroes' Middle Commentary on Aristotle's* Categories *and* De interpretatione. Trans. Charles E. Butterworth. Princeton: Princeton University Press, 1983.]

Ayras Carpancho. *Le poesie di Ayras Carpancho.* Ed. Vincenzo Minervini. Pubblicazioni della Sezione Romanza; Testi 7. Naples: Istituto Universitario Orientale, 1974.

Baer, Yitzhak. *A History of the Jews in Christian Spain*. Trans. Louis Schoffman. 2 vols. Philadelphia: Jewish Publication Society of America, 1961.

Bakhtin, M. M. *The Dialogic Imagination: Four Essays*. Ed. Michael Holquist. Trans. Caryl Emerson and Michael Holquist. Austin: University of Texas Press, 1981.

———. *Rabelais and His World*. Trans. Hélène Iswolsky. Bloomington: Indiana University Press, 1984.

Barrientos, Lope de. "Tratado de adivinanza." *Vida y obras de Fr. Lope de Barrientos*. Ed. Luis G. Alonso Getino. Anales Salmantinos. 2 vols. Salamanca: Establecimiento Tipográfico de Calatrava, 1927. Vol. 1, 87–179.

Bataille, Georges. *L'érotisme*. Paris: Minuit, 1957. [English trans.: *Erotism: Death & Sensuality*. Trans. Mary Dalwood. San Francisco: City Lights, 1986.]

Baubeta, Patricia Anne Odber de. "Superstition, or the Significance of the Sneeze." *Anticlerical Satire in Medieval Portuguese Literature*. Lewiston: Mellen, 1992.

Baudrillard, Jean. *L'échange symbolique et la mort*. Paris: Gallimard, 1976.

Bec, Pierre. *Burlesque et obscénité chez les troubadours: pour une approche du contretexte médiéval*. Paris: Stock, 1984.

Bellón Cazabán, Juan Alfredo and Pablo Jauralde Pou, eds. *Cancionero de obras de burlas provocantes a risa*. Madrid: Akal, 1974.

Beltrán, Vicente. "Dobre." *Dicionário da Literatura Galego-Portuguesa*. Eds. Giulia Lanciani and Giuseppe Tavani. Lisboa: Caminho, 1993. 219–220.

Benveniste, Émile. "La blasphémie et l'euphémie." *Problèmes de linguistique générale*. 2 vols. Paris: Gallimard, 1966–1974. Vol. 2, 255–257.

———. "Remarques sur le fonction du langage dans la découverte freudienne." *Problèmes de linguistique générale*. 2 vols. Paris: Gallimard, 1966–1974. Vol. 1, 75–87.

Bergson, Henri. *Le rire: essai sur la signification du comique*. Paris: Presses Universitaries de France, 1972.

Bershas, Henry N. *Puns on Proper Names in Spanish*. Detroit: Wayne State University Press, 1961.

Biblia sacra iuxta vulgatam versionem. Eds. Bonifatius Fischer et al. Stuttgart: Deutsche Bibelgesellschaft, 1969.

Black, Deborah L. *Logic and Aristotle's Rhetoric and Poetics in Medieval Arabic Philosophy*. Leiden: Brill, 1990.

Blackmore, Josiah. "Locating the Obscene: Approaching a Poetic Canon." *La Corónica* 26.2 (1998): 9–16.

Bloch, Marc Leopold Benjamin. *Les rois thaumaturges: étude sur le caractère surnaturel attribué à la puissance royale particulièrement en France et en Angleterre.* Paris: Gallimard, 1983.

Boswell, John. *Christianity, Social Tolerance, and Homosexuality.* Chicago: University of Chicago Press, 1982.

Bouhdiba, Abdelwahab. *La sexualité en Islam.* Paris: Presses Universitaires de France, 1975. [English trans.: *Sexuality in Islam.* Trans. Alan Sheridan. London: Routledge & Kegan Paul, 1985.]

Braga, Martín de. *Sermón contra las supersticiones rurales (De correctione rusticorum).* Barcelona: El Albir, 1981.

Branco, António Manuel. "O 'Obsceno' en Afonso X: Espaço Privilegiado do Exercicio Literário." *Colóquio/Letras,* 115–116 (1990): 65–72.

Brea Hernández, Ângelo José. " 'Se eu podesse desamar,' de Pero da Ponte: um exemplo de 'mala cansó' na lírica galego-portuguesa?" See *O Cantar dos trobadores* 351–372.

Brea, Mercedes. "La parasíntesis en las *Cantigas d'escarnho e de mal dizer.*" *Verba* 4 (1977): 127–136.

Bueno, Julián L. "La 'troba caçurra' de Juan Ruiz: parodia litúrgica." *Romance Notes* 21 (1981): 366–370.

Burke, James F. "Virtue and Sin, Reward and Punishment in the *Cantigas de Santa María.*" See Katz and Keller, *Studies on the* Cantigas de Santa María. 247–252.

———. "Again *Cruz,* the Baker-Girl: *Libro de buen amor,* ss. 115–120." *Revista Canadiense de Estudios Hispánicos* 4 (1980): 253–270.

Burns, R. "Renegades, Adventurers, and Sharp Businessmen: The Thirteenth-Century Spaniard in the Cause of Islam." *Catholic Historical Review* 58 (1972): 341–366.

Burshatin, Israel. "The Moor in the Text: Metaphor, Emblem, and Silence." *Critical Inquiry* 12 (1985). *"Race," Writing, and Difference.* Ed. Henry Louis Gates, Jr. 98–118.

Calderón de la Barca, Pedro. *El médico de su honra.* Ed. D. W. Cruickshank. Madrid: Castalia, 1987.

Callcott, Frank. *The Supernatural in Early Spanish Literature.* New York: Instituto de las Españas, 1923.

Campos, Augusto de. "Os poetas malditos do mal dizer." *Grial* 13 (1966): 357–362.

Cancioneiro da Biblioteca Nacional (Colocci-Brancuti) Cod. 10991. Lisboa: Biblioteca Nacional, 1982.

Cano Ballesta, Juan. "Los 'cantares caçurros' como género juglaresco." *La juglaresca: actas del I congreso internacional sobre la juglaresca*. Ed. Manuel Criado de Val. Madrid: EDI-6, 1986. 327–335.

————. "¿Pretende casarse la serrana de Tablada?" *La Corónica* 23:1 (1994): 3–11.

O Cantar dos trobadores: Actas do Congreso celebrado en Santiago de Compostela entre os días 26 e 29 de abril de 1993. Santiago de Compostela: Xunta de Galicia, 1993.

Cardini, Franco. *Magia, brujería y superstición en el Occidente medieval*. Trans. Antonio-Prometeo Moya. Historia, Ciencia, Sociedad, 172. Barcelona: Península, 1982.

Carmona, Fernando and Francisco J. Flores, eds. *La lengua y la literatura en tiempos de Alfonso X. Actas del Congreso Internacional (Murcia, 5–10 de marzo de 1984)*. Murcia: Departamento de Literaturas Románicas, Universidad de Murcia, 1985.

Carpenter, Dwayne E. *Alfonso X and the Jews: An Edition of and Commentary on Siete Partidas 7.24 "De los judíos."* Berkeley: University of California Press, 1986.

————. "Alfonso X el Sabio y los moros: algunas precisiones legales, históricas y textuales con respecto a *Siete partidas* 7.25." *Al-Qanṭara* 7 (1986): 229–252.

Carreño, Antonio, ed. *Actas do Segundo Congreso de Estudios Galegos. Proceedings of the Second Galician Congress (Brown University, novembro 10–12, 1988)*. Homenaxe a José Amor y Vázquez. Vigo: Galaxia, 1991.

Casas Rigall, Juan. *Agudeza y retórica en la poesía amorosa de cancionero*. Santiago de Compostela: Universidade de Santiago de Compostela, 1995.

Castro, Américo. *La realidad histórica de España*. 8th ed. México: Porrúa, 1982 [1954].

CBN. See *Cancioneiro da Biblioteca Nacional*.

Cejador y Frauca, Julio, ed. *Libro de buen amor*. By Juan Ruiz. 2 vols. Madrid: La Lectura, 1913.

Cela, Camilo José. *Diccionario secreto*. 3 vols. Madrid: Alianza, 1989.

Cerquiglini, Jacqueline. "Polysémie, ambiguïté et équivoque dans la théorie et la pratique poétiques du Moyen Age français." See Rosier, *L'ambiguïté*. 167–180.

Cervantes, Miguel de. *El ingenioso hidalgo Don Quijote de la Mancha.* Ed. Martín de Riquer. Barcelona: Planeta, 1990.

CEM. See Lapa, *Cantigas d'Escarnho e de Mal Dizer.*

Chevalier, Maxime. *Quevedo y su tiempo: la agudeza verbal.* Barcelona: Crítica, 1992.

Coopland, G. W. *Nicole Oresme and the Astrologers: A Study of His Livre de divinacions.* Cambridge: Harvard University Press, 1952.

Corominas, Joan. *Diccionario crítico y etimológico castellano y hispánico.* 6 vols. Madrid: Gredos, 1980–1991.

Correas, Gonzalo. *Vocabulario de refranes y frases proverbiales.* Ed. Víctor Infantes. Madrid: Visor, 1992.

Craddock, Jerry R. "The Legislative Works of Alfonso el Sabio." *Emperor of Culture: Alfonso X the Learned of Castile and the Thirteenth-Century Renaissance.* Ed. Robert I. Burns. Philadephia: University of Pennsylvania Press, 1990. 182–197, 257–260.

Criado de Val, Manuel. *Diccionario de español equívoco.* Madrid: EDI-6, 1981.

"Crónica del Rey don Alfonso Décimo." *Crónicas de los Reyes de Castilla.* 2 vols. Ed. Cayetano Rosell. Biblioteca de Autores Españoles 66. Madrid: Atlas, 1953. 1: 1–66.

CSM. See Alfonso X el Sabio, *Cantigas de Santa María.*

Curtius, Ernst Robert. *European Literature and the Latin Middle Ages.* London: Routledge, 1953.

D'Heur, Jean Marie. "*L'art de trouver* du chansonnier Colocci-Brancuti." *Arquivos do Centro Cultural Português* 9 (1975): 321–398. [Repr. in *Recherches internes sur la lyrique amoureuse des troubadours galiciens-portugais (XIIe-XIVe siècles: Contribution à l'étude du "corpus des troubadours".* N.p.: n.p., 1975. 97–171.]

———. *Troubadours d'Oc et troubadours galicien-portugais: recherches sur quelques échanges dans la littérature de l'Europe au Moyen Age.* Cultura medieval e moderna, 1. Paris: Fundação Calouste Gulbenkian, Centro Cultural Português, 1973.

Dagenais, John. "*Cantigas d'escarnho* and *serranillas:* The Allegory of Careless Love." *Bulletin of Hispanic Studies* (1991): 247–263.

———. *The Ethics of Reading in Manuscript Culture: Glossing the* Libro de buen amor. Princeton: Princeton University Press, 1994.

Del Castillo, Hernando. *Cancionero general de Hernando del Castillo*. Ed. José Antonio de Balenchana. 2 vols. Madrid: Bibliófilos Españoles, 1882. Vol. 1.

De Lope, Monique. *Traditions populaires et textualité dans le "Libro de buen amor."* Montpellier: Centre d'Études et de Recherches Sociocritiques, Université Paul Valéry, 1984.

De Man, Paul. "Shelley Disfigured." *The Rhetoric of Romanticism*. New York: Columbia University Press, 1984. 93–123.

De la Vega, Celestino F. *O segredo do humor*. 2nd ed. Vigo: Galaxia, 1983.

Derrida, Jacques. "White Mythology: Metaphor in the Text of Philosophy." *New Literary History* 6 (1974): 5–74.

Desbordes, Françoise. "Homonymie et synonymie d'après les textes théoriques latins." See Rosier, *L'ambiguïté*. 51–102.

Diogo, Americo Lindeza. *Sátira Galego-Portuguesa: Textos, Contextos, Metatextos*. 2 vols. Doctoral Thesis, Universidade do Minho, Braga, 1992.

Dundes, Alan. *Cracking Jokes: Studies of Sick Humor Cycles and Stereotypes*. Berkeley: Ten Speed, 1987.

Eco, Umberto. *Six Walks in the Fictional Woods*. Cambridge: Harvard University Press, 1994.

Edel, Abraham. *Aristotle and His Philosophy*. Chapel Hill: University of North Carolina Press, 1982.

Espronceda, José de. *El estudiante de Salamanca*. Madrid: Espasa-Calpe, 1982.

Fahd, Toufic. *La divination arabe: études religieuses, sociologiques et folkloriques sur le milieu natif de l'Islam*. Leiden: Brill, 1966.

Fernán Paez de Talamancos. *As cantigas de Fernán Paez de Tamalancos: edición crítica, introducción, notas e glosário*. Santiago de Compostela: Laiovento, 1992.

Ferreira, Ana Paula. "A 'Outra Arte' das Soldadeiras." *Luso-Brazilian Review*, 30 (1993): 155–166.

Filgueira Valverde, José. "La 'Seguida' medieval en la transmisión de melodías." See Carreño, *Actas*. 125–134.

——. *Sobre lírica gallega medieval y sus perduraciones*. Valencia: Bello, 1977.

Filios, Denise K. "Jokes on *Soldadeiras* in the *Cantigas de Escarnio e de Mal Dizer.*" *La Corónica* 26.2 (1998): 29–39.

Flandrin, Jean Louis. *Un temps pour embrasser: aux origines de la morale sexuelle occidentale (VIe–XIe siècle)*. Paris: Seuil, 1983.

Foucault, Michel. "Droit de mort et pouvoir sur la vie." *La volonté du savior. Histoire de la sexualité*, 1. Paris: Gallimard, 1976. 177–211.

———. *The Order of Things: An Archaeology of the Human Sciences*. New York: Vintage, 1970.

———. "Préface à la transgression." Homage à Georges Bataille. *Critique* 19 (1963): 751–769. [English trans.: "A Preface to Transgression." *Language, Counter-Memory, Practice: Selected Essays and Interviews*. Ed. Donald F. Bouchard. Trans. Donald F. Bouchard and Sherry Simon. Ithaca: Cornell University Press, 1977. 29–52.]

French, Roger. "Astrology in Medical Practice." See Garcia-Ballester et al., *Practical Medicine*. 30–59.

Fried, Debra. "Rhyme Puns." *On Puns: The Foundation of Letters*. Ed. Jonathan Culler. Oxford: Blackwell, 1988. 83–99.

Freud, Sigmund. "Humour." Ed. and trans. James Strachey. *The Standard Edition of the Complete Psychological Works of Sigmund Freud*. London: Hogarth Press, 1953–1974. Vol. 21, 161–66.

———. *Jokes and their Relation to the Unconscious*. Trans. James Strachey. New York: Norton, 1960.

———. "On the Antithetical Meaning of Primal Words." Ed. and trans. James Strachey. *The Standard Edition of the Complete Psychological Works of Sigmund Freud*. London: Hogarth Press, 1953–1974. Vol. 11, 155–61.

———. *The Psychopathology of Everyday Life*. Ed. and trans. James Strachey. New York: Norton, 1965.

———. *Totem and Taboo*. Ed. and trans. James Strachey. *The Standard Edition of the Complete Psychological Works of Sigmund Freud*. London: Hogarth Press, 1953–1974. Vol. 13, 1–161.

Gabrieli, Francesco. *Arab Historians of the Crusades*. Trans. E. J. Castello. London: Routledge, 1969.

García-Ballester, Luis, Roger French, Jonh Arrizabalaga, and Andrew Cunningham, eds. *Practical Medicine from Salerno to the Black Death*. Cambridge: Cambridge University Press, 1994.

García-Ballester, Luis. "A Marginal Learned Medical World: Jewish, Muslim and Christian Medical Practitioners, and the Use of Arabic Medical Sources in Late Medieval Spain." See García-Ballester et al., *Practical Medicine*. 353–394.

———. *La minoría musulmana y morisca*. Historia social de la medicina en España de los siglos XIII al XVI, 1. Madrid: Akal, 1976.

Garrosa Resina, Antonio. *Magia y superstición en la literatura castellana medieval.* Biblioteca de Castilla y León; Literatura, 1. Valladolid: Universidad de Valladolid, 1987.

Glick, Thomas F. *Islamic and Christian Spain in the Early Middle Ages.* Princeton: Princeton University Press, 1979.

Gombrich, E. H. "Verbal Wit as a Paradigm of Art: The Aesthetic Theories of Sigmund Freud (1856–1939)." *Tributes: Interpreters of Our Cultural Traditions.* Oxford: Phaidon, 1984. 92–115, 256.

Gonçalves, Elsa and Maria Ana Ramos. *A Lírica Galego-Portuguesa (Textos Escolhidos).* Textos Literários, 32. 2nd ed. Lisboa: Comunicação, 1985.

Goytisolo, Juan. *Señas de identidad.* Barcelona: Seix Barral, 1980.

Grace, Lee Ann. "Multiple Symbolism in the *Libro de buen amor:* The Erotic in the Forces of don Carnal." *Hispanic Review* 43 (1975): 371–380.

Gracián, Baltasar. *Agudeza y arte de ingenio.* Buenos Aires: Espasa-Calpe, 1942.

Granjel, Luis S. *La medicina española antigua y medieval.* Historia General de la Medicina Española, 1. Salamanca: Universidad de Salamanca, 1981.

Green, Monica H. "Documenting Medieval Women's Medical Practice." See García-Ballester et al., *Practical Medicine.* 322–352.

Greenblatt, Stephen J. "Learning to Curse: Aspects of Linguistic Colonialism in the Sixteenth Century." *Learning to Curse: Essays in Early Modern Culture.* New York: Routledge, 1990. 16–39.

Grimes, Larry M. *El tabú lingüístico en México: el lenguaje erótico de los mexicanos.* New York: Bilingual Press, 1978.

Guiraud, Pierre. *Sémiologie de la sexualité: essai de glosso-analyse.* Paris: Payot, 1978.

Harvey, L. P. *Islamic Spain: 1250 to 1500.* Chicago: University of Chicago Press, 1990. 31–37.

Hermes, Eberhard, ed. *The 'Disciplina Clericalis' of Petrus Alfonsi.* Trans. P. R. Quarrie. Berkeley and Los Angeles: University of California Press, 1970.

Hernández, José. *Martín Fierro.* Ed. E. F. Tiscornia. Buenos Aires: Losada, 1941.

Hernández Serna, Joaquín. "Erotismo y religiosidad en el cancionero de burlas galaico-portugués." See Carmona and Flores, *La lengua y la literatura en tiempos de Alfonso X.* 263–294.

Hicks, Eric, ed. *Le débat sur le Roman de la Rose.* Paris: Champion, 1977.

Ibn Quzmān. *Cancionero andalusí.* Trans. Federico Corriente. Madrid: Hiperión, 1989.

——. *Gramática, métrica y texto del cancionero hispanoárabe de Aban Quzmán*. Ed. F. Corriente. Madrid: Instituto Hispano-Árabe de Cultura, 1980.

Ilvonen, Eero. *Parodies de thèmes pieux dans la poésie française du Moyen Age*. Helsingförs: Société de Littérature Finnoise, 1914.

Isidoro de Sevilla. *Etimologías*. Eds. José Oroz Reta and Manuel-A. Marcos Casquero. 2 vols. Biblioteca de Autores Cristianos 433–434. Madrid: Católica, 1982–1983.

Jackson, Gabriel. *The Making of Medieval Spain*. London: Thames, 1972. [Spanish trans.: *Introducción a la España medieval*. Madrid: Alianza, 1988.]

Jacquart, Danielle and Claude Thomasset. *Sexualité et savoir médical au Moyen Age*. Paris: Presses Universitaires de France, 1985. [English trans.: *Sexuality and Medicine in the Middle Ages*. Trans. Matthew Adamson. Princeton: Princeton University Press, 1988.]

Jensen, Frede, ed. and trans. *Medieval Galician-Portuguese Poetry: An Anthology*. Garland Library of Medieval Literature, Series A, 87. New York and London: Garland, 1992.

Johan Airas de Santiago. *El cancionero de Johan Airas de Santiago, edición y estudio*. Ed. José Luis Rodríguez. *Verba*, anexo 12. Santiago de Compostela: Universidad de Santiago de Compostela, 1980.

Juan Manuel. *Libro de los enxiemplos del Conde Lucanor e de Patronio*. Ed. Alfonso I. Sotelo. Madrid: Cátedra, 1988.

Juan Ruiz. *Libro de buen amor*. Ed. Joan Corominas. Madrid: Gredos, 1973. [English trans.: See Migani and Di Cesare].

Katz, Israel J., John E. Keller et al., eds. *Studies on the* Cantigas de Santa Maria: *Art, Music, and Poetry: Proceedings of the International Symposium on the* Cantigas de Santa Maria *of Alfonso X, el Sabio [1221–1284] in Commemoration of Its 700th Anniversary Year — 1981 (New York, November 19–21)*. Madison: Hispanic Seminary of Medieval Studies, 1987.

Laín, Milagro. "De Alfonso el Sabio, 'Non me posso pagar tanto' ¿cantiga autobiográfica?" *Organizaciones textuales (textos hispánicos): Actas del III Simposio del Seminaire d'Études Littéraires de l'Université de Toulouse-Le Mirail (Toulouse, mayo de 1980)*. Toulouse: Université de Toulouse-Le Mirail, 1981.

Lanciani, Giulia and Giuseppe Tavani. *As cantigas de escarnio*. Vigo: Edicións Xerais de Galicia, 1995.

Lapa, Manuel Rodrigues, ed. *Cantigas d'Escarnho e de Mal Dizer dos Cancioneiros*

Medievais Galego-Portugueses. Rev. ed. [Vigo]: Galaxia, 1970 (1st ed. 1965). [Repr. 3rd ed. Lisboa: João Sá da Costa; Vigo: Ir Indo, 1995.]

―――. *Lições de Literatura Portuguesa: Época Medieval.* Coimbra: Coimbra Editora, 1942.

Lapesa, Rafael. "El tema de la muerte en el *Libro de buen amor.*" *Estudios dedicados a James Homer Herriot.* Madison: University of Wisconsin Press, 1966. 127–144.

Lausberg, Heinrich. *Manual de retórica literaria.* Trans. José Pérez Riesco. 3 vols. Madrid: Gredos, 1966.

Le Gentil, Pierre. *La poésie lyrique espagnole et portugaise à la fin du Moyen Age.* 2 vols. Rennes: Plihon, 1949–1953.

Le Goff, Jacques. *Time, Work and Culture in the Middle Ages.* Trans. Arthur Goldhammer. Chicago: University of Chicago Press, 1980.

Lesser, Arlene T. *La pastorela medieval hispánica: pastorelas y serranas galaico-portuguesas.* Vigo: Galaxia, 1970.

Lévi-Provençal, É. *La civilización árabe en España.* 6th ed. Madrid: Espasa-Calpe, 1982.

Liu, Benjamin. "Risabelha: A Poetics of Laughter?" *La Corónica* 26.2 (1998): 41–48.

Lopes, Graça Videira. *A Sátira nos Cancioneiros Medievais Galego-Portugueses.* Imprensa Universitária, 102. Lisboa: Estampa, 1994.

López Estrada, Francisco, ed. *Las poéticas castellanas de la Edad Media.* Madrid: Taurus, 1984.

Lorris, Guillaume de and Jean de Meun. *Le Roman de la Rose.* Ed. Daniel Poirion. Paris: Garnier-Flammarion, 1974.

Lote, Georges. *La vie et l'oeuvre de François Rabelais.* Paris: Droz, 1938.

Lourie, Elena. "Anatomy of Ambivalence: Muslims under the Crown of Aragon in the Late Thirteenth Century." *Crusade and Colonisation: Muslims, Christians and Jews in Medieval Aragon.* Aldershot, Hampshire: Variorum, 1990. Chap. 7.

Maalouf, Amin. *Les croisades vues par les Arabes.* Paris: J.-C. Lattès, 1983.

Machado, José Pedro. *Dicionário Etimológico da Língua Portuguesa.* 5 vols. Lisboa: Horizonte, 1977.

Madero, Marta. *Manos violentas, palabras vedadas: la injuria en Castilla y León (siglos XIII–XV).* Madrid: Taurus, 1992.

Maimonides. *Maimonides' Treatise on Logic (Maḳālah fi-ṣināʿat al-manṭiḳ): The*

Original Arabic and Three Hebrew Translations. Ed. and trans. Israel Efros. New York: American Academy for Jewish Research, 1938.

Makdisi, George. *The Rise of Colleges: Institutions of Learning in Islam and the West.* Edinburgh: Edinburgh University Press, 1981.

Mañach, Jorge. *Indagación del choteo.* 2nd ed. La Habana: Verónica, 1940.

Márquez Villanueva, Francisco. "The Alfonsine Cultural Concept." *Alfonso X of Castile, the Learned King (1221–1284): An International Symposium, Harvard University, 17 November 1984.* Eds. Francisco Márquez Villanueva and Carlos Alberto Vega. Harvard Studies in Romance Languages 43. Cambridge: Dept. of Romance Languages and Literatures of Harvard University, 1990.

———. "La buenaventura de Preciosa." *Nueva Revista de Filología Hispánica* 34 (1985–86): 741–768.

———. "El carnaval de Juan Ruiz." *DICENDA: Cuadernos de Filología Hispánica* (Arcadia: Estudios y textos dedicados a Francisco López Estrada) 6 (1987): 177–188.

———. *El concepto cultural alfonsí.* Madrid: Mapfre, 1994.

———. "Las lecturas del deán de Cádiz en una *cantiga de mal dizer.*" *Cuadernos Hispanoamericanos* 395 (1983): 331–345. Repr.: See Katz and Keller, *Studies on the Cantigas de Santa Maria,* 329–354.

———. *Orígenes y sociología del tema celestinesco.* Barcelona: Anthropos, 1993.

———. "Pan 'pudendum muliebris' y *Los españoles en Flandes.*" *Hispanic Studies in Honor of Joseph H. Silverman.* Ed. Joseph V. Ricapito. Newark, Delaware: Juan de la Cuesta, 1987. 247–269.

Marroni, Giovanna, ed. "Le poesie di Pedr'Amigo de Sevilha." *Istituto Universitario Orientale. Annali (Sezione Romanza)* 10 (1968): 189–339.

Marteau, Robert. "L'éros universel des alchimistes." *L'Érotisme au Moyen Âge.* Ed. Bruno Roy. Montréal: L'Aurore, 1977. 12–19.

Martin Moya. *Poesie.* Ed. Luciana Stegnano Picchio. Roma: Ateneo, 1968.

Martin Soares. *As poesías de Martin Soares.* Ed. Valeria Bertolucci. Trans. Ernesto Xosé González Seoane. Xograres e Trobadores. Vigo: Galaxia, 1992.

Martins, Mário. *A Sátira na Literatura Medieval Portuguesa (Séculos XIII e XIV).* Biblioteca Breve, 8. Lisboa: Instituto de Cultura Portuguesa, Ministerio da Educação e Investigação Científica, 1977.

May, T. E. *Wit of the Golden Age: Articles on Spanish Literature.* Teatro del Siglo de Oro, Estudios de Literatura, 2. Kassel: Reichenberger, 1986.

Mayer, Hans Eberhard. *The Crusades*. Trans. John Gillingham. Oxford: Oxford University Press, 1988.

McKeon, Richard. "Rhetoric in the Middle Ages." *Speculum* 17 (1942): 1–32.

McVaugh, Michael R. *Medicine Before the Plague: Practitioners and their Patients in the Crown of Aragon, 1285–1345*. Cambridge: Cambridge University Press, 1992.

Ménager, Daniel. *La Renaissance et le rire*. Paris: Presses Universitaires de France, 1995.

Meneghetti, María Luisa. "Una *serrana* per Marcabru?" See *O Cantar dos trobadores*, 187–198.

Menéndez Pelayo, Marcelino. *Historia de los heterodoxos españoles*. 2 vols. México: Porrúa, 1982–1983.

Menéndez Pidal, Ramón, ed. *Cantar de mio Cid: texto, gramática y vocabulario*. 3 vols. Madrid: Espasa-Calpe, 1977.

———. *Flor nueva de romances viejos*. Madrid: Espasa-Calpe, 1976.

———. *Orígenes del español: estado lingüístico de la península ibérica hasta el siglo XI*. 4th ed. Madrid: Espasa-Calpe, 1956.

———. *Poesía árabe y poesía europea*. Madrid: Espasa-Calpe, 1963.

———. *Poesía juglaresca y juglares: aspectos de la historia literaria y cultural de España*. Madrid: Espasa-Calpe, 1969.

Mérida, Rafael M. " 'D'ome atal coita nunca viu cristão': amores nefandos en los trovadores gallego-portugueses." See *O Cantar dos trobadores* 433–437.

Mettmann, Walter. "Zu Text und Inhalt der altportugiesischen *Cantigas d'escarnho e de mal dizer*." *Zeitschrift für Romanische Philologie* 82 (1966): 308–319.

Meyerson, Mark D. "Prostitution of Muslim Women in the Kingdom of Valencia: Religious and Sexual Discrimination in a Medieval Plural Society." *The Medieval Mediterranean: Cross-Cultural Contacts*. Medieval Studies at Minnesota 3. St. Cloud, MN: North Star, 1988. 87–95.

Michaëlis de Vasconcelos, Carolina, ed. *Cancioneiro da Ajuda*. 2 vols. Halle: Niemeyer, 1904. [Repr. Lisboa: Imprensa Nacional, Casa da Moeda, 1990.]

———. "Mestre Giraldo e os seus Tratados de Alveitaria e Cetraria." *Revista Lusitana* 13 (1910): 149–432.

Migani, Rigo and Mario A. Di Cesare, trans. *The Book of Good Love*. By Juan Ruiz. Albany: State University of New York Press, 1970.

Migne J.-P., ed. *Patrologia Latina*. 221 vols. Paris, 1844–1864.

Molina, Rodrigo A. "La copla cazurra del Arcipreste de Hita: hipótesis interpretiva." *Ínsula* 288 (1970): 10–11.

Monroe, James T. *Hispano-Arabic Poetry: A Student Anthology.* Berkeley and Los Angeles: University of California Press, 1974.

———. "Prolegómenos al estudio de Ibn Quzmân: el poeta como bufón." *Nueva Revista de Filología Hispánica* 34 (1985–86): 769–799.

Murphy, James J. *Rhetoric in the Middle Ages: A History of Rhetorical Theory from Saint Augustine to the Renaissance.* Berkeley and Los Angeles: University of California Press, 1974.

Mussons Freixas, Ana María. "El escarnio de Pero Meéndez da Fonseca." See Carmona and Flores, *La lengua y la literatura en tiempos de Alfonso X.* 393–414.

Nepaulsingh, Colbert I. "Sic et Non: Logic and Liturgical Tradition." *Towards a History of Literary Composition in Medieval Spain.* Toronto: University of Toronto Press, 1986. 125–160.

New Catholic Encyclopedia. New York: McGraw-Hill, 1967.

Nirenberg, David. *Communities of Violence: Persecution of Minorities in the Middle Ages.* Princeton: Princeton University Press, 1996.

Nodar Manso, Francisco. "El carácter dramático-narrativo del escarnio y maldecir de Alfonso X." *Revista Canadiense de Estudios Hispánicos* 9 (1985): 405–421.

———. "La parodia de la literatura heroica y hagiográfica en las cantigas de escarnio y mal decir." *DICENDA: Cuadernos de Filología Hispánica* 9 (1990): 151–161.

———. "El uso literario de la estructura del signo genital: onomástico y alegoría en las cantigas de escarnio." *Verba: Anuario Galego de Filoloxía* 16 (1989): 451–457.

Norenha, Ramom Reimunde. "Possíveis influências da lírica provençal na lírica galego-portuguesa concretamente na cantiga d'amor e nas chamadas 'obscenas')." *Actas do I Congresso Internacional da língua galego-portuguesa na Galiza (Ourense, 20–24 Setembro 1984).* A Corunha: AGAL [Associaçom Galega da Língua], 1986. 691–719.

Nunes, J. J. "Don Pero Gómez Barroso, trovador português do século XIII." *Boletín de la Real Academia Gallega,* 11–12 (1919–1920): 265–268, 321–325; 7–10.

O'Callaghan, Joseph F. "Image and Reality: The King Creates His Kingdom." *Emperor of Culture: Alfonso X the Learned of Castile and His Thirteenth-Century*

Renaissance. Ed. Robert I. Burns. Philadelphia: University of Pennsylvania Press, 1990. 14–32, 216–220.

Oliveira, António Resende de. *Xograres e trovadores: contexto histórico.* Trans. Valentín Arias. Vigo: Xerais, 1995.

Oring, Elliott. *Jokes and their Relations.* Lexington: University Press of Kentucky, 1992.

Osório, Jorge A. "'Cantiga de Escarnho' Galego-Portuguesa: Sociologia ou Poética?" *Revista da Faculdade de Letras do Porto* (Línguas e Literaturas), 2nd ser., 3 (1986):153–197.

Otis, Leah Lydia. *Prostitution in Medieval Society: The History of an Urban Institution in Languedoc.* Chicago: University of Chicago Press, 1985.

Pais, Marco Antonio de Oliveira. *A lírica galego-portuguesa nos séculos XIII–XIV: realidade histórica e inversão.* Doctoral Thesis, Universidade de Santiago de Compostela, 1990.

Paredes, Juan. *El cancionero profano de Alfonso X el Sabio.* Romanica Vulgaria, 10. L'Aquila: Japadre, 2001.

———. *Las cantigas de escarnio y maldecir de Alfonso X: problemas de interpretación y crítica textual.* (Papers of the Medieval Hispanic Research Seminar, 22.) London: Department of Hispanic Studies, Queen Mary and Westfield College, 2000.

———. "Las cantigas profanas de Alfonso X el Sabio (temática y clasificación)." See Carmona and Flores, *La lengua y la literatura en tiempos de Alfonso X.* 449–466.

———. *La guerra de Granada en las cantigas de Alfonso X el Sabio.* Granada: Universidad de Granada, 1992.

Paz, Octavio. "Los hijos de la Malinche." *El laberinto de la soledad.* México: Fondo de Cultura Económica, 1993. 72–97.

Pedro de Portugal. *Il canzoniere di Don Pedro de Portugal, conte di Barcelos.* Ed. M. Simões. L'Aquila: Japadre, 1985.

Pellegrini, Silvio and G. Marroni. *Nuovo repertorio bibliografico della prima lirica galego-portoghese (1814–1977).* Romanica Vulgaria, 3. L'Aquila: Japadre, 1981.

Pena, Xosé Ramón. *Literatura galega medieval.* 2 vols. Barcelona: Sotelo Blanco, 1986.

Pérez Firmat, Gustavo. *Literature and Liminality: Festive Readings in the Hispanic Tradition.* Durham: Duke University Press, 1986.

Pero da Ponte. *Poesías*. Ed. Saverio Panunzio. Trans. Ramón Mariño Paz. Vigo: Galaxia, 1992.

Pero Garcia Burgalês. *Les chansons de Pero Garcia Burgalês*. Ed. P. Blasco. Paris: Fundação Calouste Gulbenkian, Centro Cultural Português, 1984.

Peters, Edward. "The Systematic Condemnation of Magic in the Thirteenth Century." *The Magician, the Witch and the Law*. Philadelphia: University of Pennsylvania Press, 1978. 85–109.

Petrarca, Francesco. *Invective contra medicum: testo latino e volgarizzamento di Ser Domenico Silvestri*. Ed. Pier Giorgio Ricci. Roma: Storia e Letteratura, 1950.

Petronius. *Satyricon*. Trans. Michael Heseltine. Loeb Classical Library. Cambridge, MA: Harvard University Press, 1961.

Pimental, Alfredo, ed. *Fuero Real de Afonso X, o Sábio: Versão Portuguesa do Século XIII*. Lisboa: Instituto para a Alta Cultura, 1946.

Presilla, Maricel E. "The Image of Death and Political Ideology in the *Cantigas de Santa María*." See Katz and Keller, *Studies on the* Cantigas de Santa Maria. 403–457.

Quevedo, Francisco de. *Obras satíricas y festivas*. Madrid: Espasa-Calpe, 1975.

Ramos, Maria Ana. "La satire dans les *Cantigas d'escarnho e de mal dizer:* Les péchés de la langue." *Atalaya* 5 (1994): 67–84.

Reckert, Stephen. "La semiótica de la cantiga: cantigas medievales como significantes poéticos de significados antropológicos." *Crítica semiológica de textos literarios hispánicos: volumen 2 de las Actas del Congreso Internacional sobre Semiótica y Hispanismo celebrado en Madrid en los días del 20 al 25 de junio de 1983*. Ed. Miguel Angel Garrido Gallardo. Madrid: CSIC, 1986.

Resende, Garcia de. *Cancioneiro Geral de Garcia de Resende*. Ed. Cristina Almeida Ribeiro. Lisboa: Comunicação, 1991.

Richlin, Amy. "Invective against Women in Roman Satire." *Arethusa* 17 (1984): 67–80.

Rico, Francisco. "Brujería y literatura." *Brujología: Congreso de San Sebastian, ponencias y comunicaciones*. Madrid: Seminarios y Ediciones, 1975. 97–117.

———. "La clerecía del mester." *Hispanic Review* 53 (1985): 1–23, 127–150.

———. "Las letras latinas del siglo XII en Galicia, León y Castilla." *Ábaco* 2 (1969): 9–91.

Rodrigu'Eanes de Vasconcelos. *As cantigas de Rodrigu'Eanes de Vasconcelos*. Ed. Manuel Ferreiro. Santiago de Compostela: Laiovento, 1992.

Rodríguez, José Luís. "La cantiga de escarnio y su estructura histórico-literaria: el equívoco como recurso estilístico nuclear en la cantiga d'escarnho de los Cancioneros." *Santiago de Compostela: La ciudad, las instituciones, el hombre.* Estudios Compostelanos, 4. Santiago de Compostela: Colegio Franciscano, 1976. 33–46.

———. "A mulher nos cancioneiros: notas para um anti-retrato descortês." *Simpósio Internacional Muller e Cultura: Compostela, 27–29 de febrero de 1992.* Ed. Aurora Marco. Santiago de Compostela: Departamento de Didáctica da Língua e a Literatura, Universidade de Santiago de Compostela, 1993. 43–67.

Rojas, Fernando de. *La Celestina.* Ed. Julio Cejador y Frauca. 2 vols. Madrid: Espasa-Calpe, 1972.

Roncaglia, Aurelio. "Glanures de la critique textuelle dans le domaine de l'ancienne lyrique galego-portugaise: le *pardon* de la Balteira et le *casamento* de la 'tendeira.'" *Critique textuelle portugaise: Actes du Colloque, Paris, 20–24 octobre 1981.* Paris: Calouste Gulbenkian, 1986. 19–27.

Rosier, Irène. "Évolution des notions d'*equivocatio* et *univocatio* au XIIe siècle." See Rosier, *L'ambigüité.* 103–166.

Rosier, Irène, ed. *L'ambiguïté: cinq études historiques.* Lille: Presse Universitaire de Lille, 1988.

Rossiaud, Jacques. *Medieval Prostitution.* Trans. Lydia G. Cochrane. New York: Blackwell, 1988.

Sage, Carleton M. *Paul Albar of Cordoba: Studies on His Life and Writings.* Catholic University of America Studies in Medieval History, n. s. 5. Washington: Catholic University of America Press, 1943.

Santillana, Marqués de. *Poesías completas.* Ed. Manuel Durán. 2 vols. Madrid: Castalia, 1989. Vol. 2.

Scarborough, Connie L. "The *Cantigas de Santa María* as Penitential Text." See Carreño, *Actas.* 135–142.

Scholberg, Kenneth R. *Sátira e invectiva en la España medieval.* Madrid: Gredos, 1971.

Scott, Samuel Parsons. See Alfonso X el Sabio, *Las siete partidas.*

Servais, Jean–Jacques and Jean-Pierre Laurend. *Histoire et dossier de la prostitution.* Paris: Planète, 1965.

Shakespeare, William. "Othello." *The Riverside Shakespeare.* Boston: Houghton Mifflin, 1974.

Shatzmiller, Joseph. *Jews, Medicine, and Medieval Society*. Berkeley and Los Angeles: University of California Press, 1994.

Shell, Marc. *Money, Language, and Thought: Literary and Philosophic Economies from the Medieval to the Modern Era*. Berkeley and Los Angeles: University of California Press, 1982.

Shorter Encyclopedia of Islam. Eds. H. A. R. Gibb and J. H. Kramers. Leiden: Brill, 1991.

Siraisi, Nancy G. "The Faculty of Medicine." *Universities in the Middle Ages*. Ed. Hilde de Ridder-Symoens. A History of the University in Europe, 1. Cambridge: Cambridge University Press, 1992. 360–387.

Snow, Joseph T. *The Poetry of Alfonso X: A Critical Bibliography*. Research Bibliographies and Checklists, 19. London: Grant & Cutler, 1977.

Spade, Paul Vincent. "Synonymy and Equivocation in Ockham's Mental Language." *Journal of the History of Philosophy* 18 (1980): 9–22. Repr. in *Lies, Language and Logic in the Late Middle Ages*. London: Variorum, 1988.

Spector, Jack J. *The Aesthetics of Freud: A Study in Psychoanalysis and Art*. New York: McGraw-Hill, 1972.

Spina, Segismundo, ed. *As Cantigas de Pero Mafaldo*. Rio de Janeiro: Tempo Brasileiro, 1983.

Spitzer, Leo. "Enaziado, anaciado." *Revista de Filología Hispánica* 7 (1945): 160–162.

Summa pulsuum. Trans. Michael R. McVaugh. *A Sourcebook of Medieval Science*. Ed. Edward Grant. Cambridge: Harvard University Press, 1974. 745–748.

Tavani, Giuseppe. "La *cantiga d'escarnho e de mal dizer* galego-portoghese." *Grundriss der Romanischen Literaturen des Mittelalters* 6. (La littérature didactique, allégorique et satirique.) Ed. Hans Robert Jauss. Heidelberg: Winter, 1968–70. 309–313.

———. "O Cómico e o Carnavalesco nas Cantigas de Escarnho e Maldizer." *Boletím de Filología* 29 (1984): 59–74.

———. *A poesía lírica galego-portuguesa*. Trans. Rosario Álvarez Blanco and Henrique Monteagudo. 3rd ed. Vigo: Galaxia, 1991.

———. "La satira morale e letteraria nella lirica galego-portoghese." *Grundriss der Romanischen Literaturen des Mittelalters* 6. (La littérature didactique, allégorique et satirique.) Ed. Hans Robert Jauss. Heidelberg: Winter, 1968–70. 272–274.

————. "L'ultimo periodo della lirica galego-portoghese: archiviazione di un' esperienza poetica." *Revista da Biblioteca Nacional* 3 (1983): 9–17.

Todorov, Tzvetan, ed. "El cruzamiento entre culturas." *Cruce de culturas y mestizaje cultural.* Trans. Antonio Desmonts. Madrid: Júcar, 1988. 9–31.

Torres Fontes, Juan. *Un médico alfonsí: maestre Nicolás.* Murcia: Sucesores de Nogués, 1954.

Uc Faidit. *The* Donatz Proensals *of Uc Faidit.* Ed. J. H. Marshall. London: Oxford University Press, 1969.

Usāma ibn Munqiḏ. *Kitāb al-I'tibār.* [*An Arab-Syrian Gentleman and Warrior in the Period of the Crusades.* Trans. Philip K. Hitti. 1929. Repr. in Kritzeck, James. *Anthology of Arabic Literature.* New York: Meridian, 1964. 203–204.]

Valdés, Juan de. *Diálogo de la lengua.* Ed. José F. Montesinos. Madrid: Espasa-Calpe, 1976.

Vaquero, Mercedes. "Las 'cantigas d'escarnho e de maldizer' como invectiva de la épica." See Carreño, *Actas.* 143–149.

Vasvari, Louise O. "The Battle of Flesh and Lent in the 'Libro del Arçipreste': Gastro-genital Rites of Reversal." *La Corónica* 20:1 (1991–92): 1–15.

————. "La semiología de la connotación: lectura polisémica de 'Cruz cruzada panadera.'" *Nueva Revista de Filología Hispánica* 32 (1983): 299–324.

Vieira, Yara Frateschi. "O Escândalo das Amas e Tecedeiras nos Cancioneiros Galego-Portugueses." *Colóquio/Letras* 76 (1983): 18–27.

Walker, Roger M. "'Con miedo de la muerte la miel non es sabrosa': Love, Sin and Death in the *Libro de buen amor.*" '*Libro de buen amor*' *Studies.* Ed. G. B. Gybbon-Monypenny. London: Tamesis, 1970.

Weiss, Julian. *The Poet's Art: Literary Theory in Castile c1400–60.* Oxford: Society for Mediaeval Languages and Literature, 1990.

Whinnom, Keith. "Hacia una interpretación y apreciación de las canciones del *Cancionero general* de 1511." *Filología* 13 (1968–69): 361–381.

Wilder, Thornton. *The Bridge of San Luis Rey.* New York: Washington Square, 1955.

Wright, William. *A Grammar of the Arabic Language.* London, 1862.

Zaid, Rhonda. "Some Adverse Criticism of Women in the *Cantigas de Santa Maria.*" *Bulletin of the Cantigueiros de Santa Maria* 2 (1988–1989): 79–88.

Ziolkowski, Jan M. "The Erotic Paternoster." *Neuphilologische Mitteilungen* 88 (1987): 31–34.

————. "The Humour of Logic and the Logic of Humour in the Twelfth-Century Renaissance." *Journal of Medieval Latin* 3 (1993): 1–26.

Zumthor, Paul. "L'équivoque generalisée." *Le masque et la lumière: la poétique des grands rhétoriqueurs.* Paris: Seuil, 1978. 267–281.